Also by Larry W. Dennis

Repeat Business

Empowering Leadership

Larry W. Dennis

Rising Tide Publishing
Portland, Oregon

Rising Tide Publishing
5440 S. W. Westgate Drive, Suite 340
Portland, Oregon 97221

Dedication

Empowering Leadership is dedicated to the empowering women in my life; my grandmother who loved me with unconditional love, my mother who knew I could never do anything wrong and my wife who has stood beside me, trusted me, and believed in me even when we couldn't pay the rent.

Foreword

All managers and leaders want positive results. A modern leader must act upon the knowledge that his or her job is to create an environment where a person's natural inclination to move forward is stimulated and the best results are actualized. The principles of synergistic teamwork taught in this book will enable you to bring out the best in your subordinates and yourself so that results actually exceed your high expectations.

Larry W. Dennis introduces one of the most powerful new management techniques in *Empowering Leadership*. Although there are many leadership techniques that have been taught over the past decades—derivations of the same basic methods in most cases—the principles in *Empowering Leadership* are unique, exciting and insightful.

Dennis' fifteen leadership principles show the reader how to win the cooperation and loyalty of the individuals on whose cooperation *real* success depends. As the author so aptly puts it, acknowledgment creates a culture which enables people to "hit home runs." Empowerment satisfies a person's basic need to be recognized, appreciated, and respected as an individual and a team member.

Few authors capture the essence of concepts that really work as well as Larry W. Dennis. I find myself re-reading page after page because his ideas are so practical and logical that they have profound significance. The examples he uses to illustrate his points are right on target. I admire Larry Dennis and his work, and this book is destined to be a classic. It should be compulsory reading at every business school in America.

Empowering Leadership is your blueprint to building a strong, effective, and dynamic management team whose members are empowered to succeed.

Charles R. Whitlock, Ph. D.
Chairman, Executive Officer Club, Inc. and
Author of *How To Get Rich, Secrets Of Successful Selling,* and *Just Do It Management.*

Table Of Contents

Leader Wanted

Leader wanted who will not lose individuality in a crowd, a leader who has the courage of his convictions and who is not afraid to say "No," though all the world says yes.

Leader wanted who is dominated by a mighty purpose. A leader who will not allow the over development of one faculty stamp out or paralyze other faculties.

Leader wanted who is larger than his calling, who considers it a low estimate of his occupation to value it merely as a means of making a living.

Leader wanted who sees self development, education, culture, discipline, character and personhood in his work.

Leader wanted who is not a coward in any part of his nature.

Leader wanted who is well balanced, who is not cursed with some small defect or weakness which cripples his usefulness and neutralizes his power.

Leader wanted who is symmetrical and not one-sided in his development, who has not spent all of his energies in one narrow specialty and allowed other branches of his life to wither and die.

Leader wanted who is broadminded and does not take a half view of things, a person who mixes common sense with intuition, who does not let a college education spoil him for practical everyday life; a leader who prefers substance to show and regards his good name as a priceless treasure.

Leader wanted who is full of life and fire, whose passions are trained to heed its strong desire, the servant of a tender conscience, who has learned to love beauty whether of nature or of art and to hate all violence and respect all others as he does himself.

Leader wanted who is educated in all ways, whose nerves are brought to a sharper sensibility, whose brain is cultured, keen, incisive, and whose hands are adept, whose eyes are alert, sensitive, microscopic and whose heart is tender, magnanimous and true.

Peter J. Daniels

Leadership

*"One person of courage
makes a majority."*
Andrew Jackson

Several years ago, when I first wrote the *Leadership Development Lab* (LDL), I needed a definition for the word Leadership. When I turned to Webster and other authoritative sources, not being satisfied with the definitions I found, I created my own. I defined leadership as "bringing out the best so results exceed high expectations." The purpose of this book is to provide you with the guidelines, insights, understanding and tools needed to help you bring out the best so your results will exceed your highest expectations. Authority can be granted through position, or title, power can be obtained through specialized knowledge, but leadership is always internally generated. Leadership is available to anyone who develops their ability to get along with, relate to, understand and motivate others.

Leaders have faith in themselves and, more importantly, in the direction they seek and the decisions they make. Nothing is impossible with leadership and self-confidence. Certainly, nothing of significance has ever been accomplished without leadership. Great movements in history are a tribute to the power of leadership. Many of the greatest accomplishments in the history of civilization have been made against "impossible" odds. Demosthenes—Columbus—Beethoven—Helen Keller—George Washington Carver—Henry Ford—Sam Walton (of Walmart)—Steve Jobs (of Apple)—Bill Gates (of Microsoft) all reached the pinnacle of success because they were determined to lead in something the world thought was impossible. True leaders believe in their vision, and this belief in their vision gives them self-confidence, and they believe in the team of which they're a part. Empowering leaders understand that they must multiply themselves through others. They must help others grow. True leaders recognize that the growth of others is a reflection of their true leadership ability.

The need for leadership as we move with lightning speed towards the 21st Century has never been greater. In large part, the vacuum in leadership is a result of the breakdown in traditional authority—the authority of parents over children, church over society, the military over nations, management over workers, men over women. This vacuum can only be filled by leadership. It's been said that leadership is the scarcest resource on our planet. Yet leadership is available to anyone who has the courage of their convictions, the confidence to exercise the risks inherent in leadership and the ability to influence others.

> *"The final test of a leader is that he leaves behind him in other men the conviction and will to carry on."*
> Walter Lippmann

If persons with character and principles do not assume leadership, there will always be those lacking principle who will be more than willing to fill the void. Today is the time when we need new imaginative, creative, innovative, caring, and effective leadership. We need new leadership in education as we notice that old methods no longer have relevance for our kids who cannot compete effectively for jobs and who record S.A.T. scores that continue to decline.

We need new leaders in politics as governments struggle to respond to bigger demands for service and have fewer financial resources. And we certainly need new leaders in business, leaders who are more concerned with the quality of their output, the competitiveness of their products and services, the long-term viability of their companies and the future of their employees than their own stock option plans and their bonuses.

We need business leaders who are not responding to quarterly profits alone. As we've watched America's standard of living steadily decline over the past 20 years we've known, perhaps without saying it loudly enough, that this decline is directly attributable to our lack of quality and productivity stemming from ineffective leadership. We continue to pioneer innovations like the VCR and then watch other nations steal the leadership role, produce the products and reap the long term profits.

The principles in this book are not limited in their application to the captains of industry, or the heads of state. This book is for anyone who understands and recognizes that in every sector of our society there is an opportunity, a vast vacuum created by a lack of leadership. I've seen it in businesses of all kinds when there have been obvious opportunities to stand up, speak out, be counted. People have turned away out of fear or lack of understanding of what an important difference they can make.

One Person Of Courage Makes A Majority

The purpose of *Empowering Leadership* is to provide you with the guidance that will enable you to fill the vacuum of leadership in your own world, allowing you to experience a greater sense of accomplishment and personal empowerment. Equally as important, is to help you know how to make your team, those with whom you associate, gain a greater sense of accomplishment and achievement from their work knowing that what they do makes a difference, counts, is appreciated—knowing that they're making a difference for the better in our world.

I've learned over the past 25 years of training thousands of leaders that empowering leaders have the ability to project their ideas into images that excite their teams, and develop those images into new ways of doing things. Empowering leaders create excitement in work.

Little Visitor

The importance of projecting images to excite people to aim toward a goal was demonstrated for me recently in a personal way when my four-year-old granddaughter, Alex, arrived for a visit from California. We were excited about her coming and sad to see her go.

What about you? Do you make everyone's life positive? Do they look forward to your coming? Maybe it's too high a standard to compare ourselves to the effervescence of a four-year-old, and certainly I wouldn't want to be responsible for being as good at making everybody's life positive as my granddaughter. Yet I know all of us can make this world a better place by adding our own optimism, our own enthusiasm, our joy. Empowering leaders bring joy, enthusiasm, and optimism into the world of those they touch, everyday. As you lift others with your joy, you lift yourself.

Empowering leaders are proactive, inspiring and willing to take the initiative. Empowering leaders have the ability to both give and get the authority and responsibility necessary to improve performance on every level. Shared ownership results in improved teamwork, enhanced production, increased profits, and greater job satisfaction for everyone involved.

Kings

You may have been granted a title which automatically gives you authority. Experience shows that regardless of the title you have been given, unless you are respected, unless you have developed your ability to "bring out the best" in others, you will never receive the degree of cooperation and enthusiastic support that is necessary for results to exceed high expectations.

While touring England several years ago, my wife and I visited Corfe Castle. The castle is a veritable fortress because of its unique positioning on the stone cliffs of England's south coast. Corfe Castle was the last stronghold on mainland England against Oliver Cromwell in the 17th Century. Lady Bankes defended the castle against Cromwell's parliamentary forces for three long years. The castle was finally taken by treachery. A supposedly loyal insider opened a back door, permitting the opposing troops to penetrate the fortress and blow it up.

You may be granted authority by position, just as the kings and queens who ruled ancient Europe. You will only experience true power when you earn the loyalty and cooperation of those who support you. Leadership is the ability to gain and retain the cooperation, loyalty and enthusiastic support of others.

Revolving Door

I met recently with the comptroller of a construction firm that specializes in a revolutionary, modern coating and production technology. As we discussed the makeup of the firm and the length of time employees had worked for the company, it became apparent that the company experienced a completely unacceptable rate of turnover among the professional staff—the persons who worked in the office closest to the president. The comptroller was quite willing to tell me why. In his opinion, the erratic, unprofessional behavior of the president and one of the key staff members was the reason. If you are the president you can get away with almost anything—or can you? We can take liberties with how we work and deal with others and get away with unskilled behavior, but in the long run, it costs us friends, relationships, loyalty and teamwork.

The action I call you to is: Get a good personal behavior coach—someone who is willing to call you on your unskillful behavior and listen to and thank him for his feedback. Change the way you relate to and with others, you'll make and keep stronger, deeper, lasting relationships and you'll gain profound personal strength through the process.

Ice Cream Cone

Jim, the owner and president of Hart, Inc., a mechanical contracting firm told me a wonderful, warm story about coaching his ten-year-old daughters little league team, the Slammers. "The ball was being thrown all over the place. No one was catching the ball, and if they did catch it they still failed to make their plays. The game was completely out of control. I thought to myself, 'I guess I am the coach. I probably ought to do something.' To be frank, at this point I wasn't sure anyone could make a difference with these girls—least of all me. I decided to apply my newly acquired coaching skills. I walked over to the first baseman and said, 'I love your enthusiasm and if you will hold your glove up high and steady before the shortstop throws the ball to provide a clear target, and put your foot on the base (clarify standards) you'll be more successful in catching the ball, tagging the runner and getting an out. We will win the game, we will have a winning team, and we can all go to Baskin-Robbins for ice cream after our win."

Amazing as it seemed to Jim, the next time the short stop scooped up the ball and started to throw, the first baseman already had her glove held up high and steady. The shortstop threw the ball right to the glove. The first baseman kept her foot on the base and they got the runner out. Yahoo!

From that point, the game changed. Jim was able to become a cheerleader with lots of "That's the way," and "Wow"—a new tempo set in. To Jim's astonishment, the Slammers did win.

The lessons we can learn from Jim's experience are:

1. The team and every team member on it needs a target—an overriding, over-arching goal—a clearly articulated, compelling vision statement: Win the game and go to Baskin-Robbins. A vision statement should pull you straight up.

2. Sub-targets need to be clear for each player: "Hold the glove high"—"Hold the glove steady"—"Keep your foot on the base."

3. Team members need to be given some helpful training: "Keep your foot on the base while holding the glove high—let me show you how." Training builds self-esteem. Training is seen as a fringe benefit; it builds moral and helps reduce turnover. Cross training helps build teamwork, esprit de corps, communication and understanding.

4. Coaching is often needed even after training in how to execute the things that need to be done to achieve the goals. "You're playing with excitement!" "You're having fun!" "Let's go!" There are many aspects of coaching. Corrective feedback and cheerleading are both important for individuals and for team performance improvement. An empowering leader sets everything in motion and keeps it moving.

Leaders must call themselves to action. They must give team members clear targets to shoot for. Hold your own targets up higher. After the company and department targets have been agreed upon, commit to them. Then define the performance standards for every department and each individual team member. As Max DuPree stated in his book, *Leadership Is An Art,* "A team of giants needs giant pitchers who throw good ideas. But every great pitcher needs an outstanding catcher. Without giant catchers, the idea of giant pitchers may eventually disappear."

This is a superb example of how important it is to make our expectations clear and to explain and document our standards for excellence. Empowering leaders make the vision clear. It's impossible for our people to read our minds and perform in the exact manner we expect and need unless we first make our expectations clear—unless we've clarified for them "What excellence looks like." I have heard countless presentations in my classes of similar examples—an employee has been with a company, often for years, getting moved from location to location, from position to position and no one has ever really clarified standards, procedures or expectations of excellence. Everyone has a right to know what excellence looks like. If excellence is not understood, excellence can't be performed.

To be an empowering leader be sure everyone on your team knows what excellence looks like. Clarify the playing field. Discuss the extent of the authority you are giving. Team members need to perform at the highest level. Be sure their authority is understood and agreed to and that accountability has been accepted. Show a clear understanding of:

... the visions and values of the company.

... the company's goals.

... the primary goal of the department.

... the primary goal of the job.

... the sub-goals of the job.

... the standards for excellence.

A policy manual, of course, is needed, but keep it thin! Give people a clear picture of what outstanding performance looks like. When your people approximate your standards of excellence, be sure to praise them, even when they are approximately right. Give them supportive feedback and encouragement. You will build a winning team.

Overtime

I had been taking the 11 pm Thursday night flight from Seattle to Portland for the last several months. Last week, as I was quick-timing down concourse A of the SeaTac Airport, I was surprised to see the little concourse bar open. I was sure that it had always been closed other evenings as I walked by. I asked Bruce, the bartender, if he always stayed open late. He said, "No, we close at 10 o'clock but we've been so busy that I just stayed open. It's fun when we are busy—a 12-hour shift goes by fast." Then he went on to say, "Besides that, my boss is on the other side of the airport, so he doesn't bother me much and that makes my job easier too."

Isn't it sad that a person enjoys his work more when the boss doesn't come around and is even willing to work longer and probably harder when the boss stays away?

The questions many leaders are asking:

... can people be motivated?

... can I motivate people?

... how do I motivate people?

... is it my job to motivate my people?

The best way I have ever found to answer these questions was to ask the top level management teams who attended our Management Team Advance the question, "What would motivate you to peak performance?" To even answer this question, these managers must admit to a lack of 100 percent motivation. That is honest. None of us is 100 percent motivated 100 percent of the time. After the participants wrote out their individual responses, we gathered the answers on an easel up front for everyone to see. Here is a list from some recent programs of what the top ten managers of 200-person manufacturing firms wanted for their own motivation:

... additional responsibility.

... acknowledgement.

... a sense of achievement.

... meaningful challenges.

... recognition for accomplishment.

... recognition from peers.

... ownership (running my own area).

... a sense of self worth.

... proper tools.

... a sense of fulfillment.

... completed effort.

... money.

... a sense of teamwork.

... recognition as being the best (feeling like a winner).

My followup question is always the same: "What do you think would motivate your team to peak performance?" The light comes on and participants begin to see that their people want what they themselves want: autonomy, authority, responsibility, permission to be creative and innovative and room to explore new ways to solve problems and improve processes. It is true: motivation, "a reason for movement," comes from within. Our job, as empowering leaders, is to get out of the way and create an environment in which people's natural inclination to move forward is stimulated and results are actualized.

Well how about you? Do you inspire, motivate, support and uplift? Or do you block, hold back, discourage and disempower others? The action I call you to is this: find a way, today, to be an encouraging, positive force for good in the lives of all of your team members.

Cooperation

One of the most important assets of empowering leaders is their ability to inspire cooperation. Many executives give this valuable quality little thought. Often, they think everybody else should cooperate with them, since they provide the direction for the company.

Actually, leadership starts when you gain the enthusiastic cooperation of others. Cooperation means two or more people involved in the operation as one: in harmony, together with the same goals needing and supporting each other.

A famous study in Cambridge, Massachusetts of several hundred prominent business executives determined that the one trait successful persons had in common was a superior ability in handling interpersonal relationships. Doesn't your own experience confirm this? Haven't you noticed that the higher an executive rises, the more time they spend with people? That's only natural. *Leadership is leading people.*

Tripping

Because leadership is so important to the success of a company, cooperation can be the key to a successful future. This was demonstrated by Mac.

Mac, the shop foreman for a major trenching company, told our Leadership Development Lab that the office staff of his company meets on a weekly basis to discuss what did and did not work in the office the week before. They also discuss upcoming projects and possible challenges. They generally look for ways to make things run more smoothly. They take the time to do problem-solving around what may not be working as effectively as it could be, and they plan for the upcoming week. This is a terrific example of cooperation.

Mac said, "A couple of weeks ago, I invited myself to their weekly office staff meeting. I just showed up, sat down, and began to participate in the meeting. I made some suggestions and shared some ideas."

Mac made a request of the office staff: "When you order supplies, rather than ordering daily, would you make one list of everything you need for the week and then make one order so our guys can make one trip during the week instead of several? This will save a lot of time and reduce frustration."

Their response was: "Sure, we can get organized and pull together a list of needed supplies for the week." And that's the way it's been working ever since.

During the meeting, Mac was able to make other important suggestions to the office team which seemed to help them find some solutions to their problems. At the end of the meeting, they invited Mac back to be a permanent part of their office staff meetings.

Mac took a stand. Mac became involved. Mac assumed the mantle of leadership—he didn't wait for it to be handed to him, he didn't wait to be invited, he didn't wait to be asked. By assuming the mantle of leadership, and through the process, he began to make an even greater contribution to his company. Certainly, Mac feels better about Mac, and the larger team feels better about the office team. Rework (extra trips for supplies) has been eliminated, and problems are being solved faster, easier synergistically.

My challenge to you is to stand up, speak out, be counted, be a part of the solution, assume the mantle of leadership (don't wait to be invited—for somebody to hand leadership to you). Don't complain about not being heard. Don't complain about not being invited. Don't complain about not being listened to. Take the risk of being rejected. Take the risk of being not listened to. Stand up, speak out and be counted. You will gain a sense of empowerment.

Pain in the Neck

Clifton told me, "Yesterday, I concluded a major presentation and then rushed out of my office to see my doctor. A few days earlier I had pinched a nerve in my neck and the pain had become too acute for me to ignore. As I drove to the doctor I thought how incredible it is that one small point of pain can hurt so much. The entire right side of my body was hurting. My concentration was down, my energy was down, and I knew I hadn't been able to support my partner in an important presentation quite the way I would have liked to. The lesson I learned is that even small pockets of pain affect the entire system. In our companies we just can't blame shipping or production when something goes wrong. We can't say, 'Boy, those guys in sales are really hurting,' without considering the affect of a sales slump on the rest of the team. When empowering leaders observe some discomfort in a team member and know something is not quite right, they act immediately. The benefit gained is a healthy, empowered, winning team."

Bullies

Nancy told our Leadership Lab: "This past October three young children from my neighborhood were shot at by a teenage bully with a pellet gun. This was just one in a series of attacks over the past couple of years by this youth and his brothers. In the past, my neighbors and I had lamented the fact that our children were being harassed, intimidated, and actually shot at and attacked. The police had been called to the home involved on several occasions; however, no permanent end to the behavior resulted.

"A neighbor and I felt frustrated by the situation and our sense of helplessness. We decided something more could be done rather than just notifying the police and talking about it. We thought it necessary to take action and get information out to our neighbors in order to allow our children to feel safe in their neighborhood. My neighbor and I made up a notice and distributed it door to door in our neighborhood. We explained the situation (some people were unaware of any problems) and set up a meeting to discuss possibilities to make our neighborhood safe. We were ecstatic with the response; over 100 people showed up for the first meeting. Once we were together action came easily. People volunteered to organize and participate in neighborhood watch walks, cellular phones were donated for use during the walks, the police became more responsive once we voiced our dissatisfaction over the past results of their actions, the school and school board became more cooperative after we organized and presented a united front.

"Three arrests occurred as a direct result of the neighborhood walks; only one incident of intimidation in the past four months, and a wonderful sense of togetherness in the neighborhood have been our rewards.

"The lesson I learned: people are willing and able to accomplish great things; it just takes a little initiative and leadership by a few; and a group is often able to accomplish more than individuals alone. The action I call you to is: to take the lead, take a chance, don't let your fears bully you around and encourage participation in things you believe in and you will get action and results. The benefit you will gain is: a better world and a great sense of satisfaction."

"Lead, follow, or get out of the way." I have no idea who first imparted this snappy bit of wisdom. It seems that I heard it for the first time 25 years ago. I have since seen it on posters, plaques, flipcharts, overheads and paperweights around the country and even around the world. It is great personal and professional advice but it doesn't tell you what you need to do to be a leader. It doesn't even define what leadership is. So far, we've looked at several definitions, but I think it is worth reviewing them again in different terms. True leaders believe in their vision and their belief gives them self confidence. True leaders understand that they must multiply themselves through others. They must help others grow. Empowering leaders recognize that the growth of others is a reflection of their true leadership ability.

Knowledge is Power

Most companies hire people for their technical knowledge and skills. Then these people are promoted into leadership roles based on their technical performance. Unfortunately, technical knowledge and experience do not equip these people with the skills to face the challenge of leading a work group, a department, or, ultimately, a company. By developing our latent leadership skills, we become a more competent resource and are able to effectively take on added responsibility.

I recently met with the head of engineering for a prominent software manufacturing firm here in the Northwest. This firm employs 400 professional engineers. While visiting with this engineering division vice president, we discussed the challenges of building a championship team and creating empowered performance at all levels.

"We hire people on the basis of where they went to school, where they've worked, their background, experience and technical expertise," he told me. "When we fire people (the firm has laid off more than 200 people in the past few weeks), we lay them off or fire them on the basis of their lack of ability to get along with, relate to, understand, work successfully with and motivate people."

He went on to say: "Normally, all advancement beyond the entry position is based, in large part, on that person's ability to work with the team, contribute successfully to the team, add to the team."

Though I have said this many times myself in many different ways, this manager put it more effectively than I have ever heard it said in the 25 years that I have been in the management development and training business. We have a tendency sometimes to think all we need is the technical training, the technical education, the technical experience, and that somehow this education entitles us to possession of responsibility and authority.

Our middle son, Barry A. Dennis, visited the Soviet Union in July 1989, just five months before the Berlin Wall came down. He told us that many of the major buildings in Moscow have the Russian equivalent of "Knowledge Is Power" inscribed above the door arches.

As a percentage of their population, the Soviets may

have had more scientists than anywhere else in the world, though it became necessary to build a wall to keep them in.

Knowledge is only power when a person knows how to apply it. It takes courage, initiative, assertiveness, vision, determination and insight to make practical use of knowledge. And, as you endeavor to apply your knowledge, it is your leadership, team-building, people and communication skills that determine your promotability and your contribution to the team. In many ways, your technical training and experience only get you through the front door.

My lesson learned, once again, is though we may worship at the seat of technical knowledge, the key to our success is our ability to get along with, understand and work successfully with other people.

The action I call you to is: Develop your ability to work even more effectively with your team, and to get along with, understand and motivate people. The benefits you will gain are the full use and value of your technical knowledge and you will experience job security and advancement.

It has been said that leadership is a lost art and that American business and industry has quit producing great leaders. We develop and promote managers, but we have not insisted that they be leaders. The power and potential of leadership, the need for leadership, exists today to a greater degree than ever before. Organizations that prosper experience extraordinary leadership and we know that an empowering leader accepts as primary the responsibility of building people and making them successful—to help them grow, develop and reach their full potential. This requires that we get to know people we work with, who work for us, and that we work for. We need to identify what their strengths are, what we can do to help them develop those strengths and make them stronger. An empowering leader is eager to help people move on to bigger and better

things, eager to help people along the way. Empowering organizations reward leaders on the basis of how many people they
have helped make achievers.

Rough Waters

I couldn't help noticing a recent headline in *The
Oregonian:* "Boat dealers optimistic about a better season." It
reminded me of talking with the owner of a Portland marina last
spring. It seems he was running a reasonably successful business. He was even featured in a newspaper article not more than
six months earlier as a successful boat dealer and businessman.
The article said that, in spite of the challenges that exist in the
retail boat business, he was succeeding. The article held him up
as an example of success in spite of tough times.

I conducted an early morning one-hour breakfast workshop as a part of his weekly company meeting not more than six
or nine months previously. It was clear to me, by the end of the
workshop, that there were many opportunities to enhance communication and teamwork, improve performance and increase
customer satisfaction.

Though he and his wife agreed their company needed
training, he made the decision at that time to "do it later," to not
do anything with us right then. Well, "later" came, and no one
participated in our training. And later came again, and still no
one participated in our training.

Later came once again, the other day, when I checked in
with him. He said: "If I can speak confidentially, Larry, we have
made a decision to sell our business. We're not going to sell the
entire business, we're just going to close out, liquidate our inventory, sell what's here that can be sold."

I can't be sure that if he and his team had participated in
our training that it would have made the required difference for

him to survive until the tide turned. I do know that there was a crying need for leadership training at the time I conducted the workshop. They were clinging to the status quo and blaming each other instead of each person taking responsibility for his own change and improvements.

This is just one more example of another over-20-year-old company going out of business. I asked him what he is going to do, and he told me that he hoped he could get a job somewhere. This story could have had a different ending, but this ending is one we see over and over again.

The owner was so stuck in "the way we have always done it," so stuck on blaming, hoping, complaining and wishing. He was literally paralyzed. He had given up on his ability to exercise leadership—on his ability to influence the direction and course of his business and, ultimately, of his life.

How about you? Are you hoping things will get better, wishing, waiting, worrying, working? Or are you innovating, creating, stimulating participating?

Replace wishing with determination; waiting with action; and worrying with positive vision and working toward real synergistic teamwork.

To help you define how you'd best like to lead, think about the persons you would most willingly follow, then make a list of the qualities they possess. What is it that attracts you to them? What is it that makes you willing or eager to follow them? What is it in them that you value? Ask yourself, "Do I need to add to my list of strengths these qualities I have identified? Are they qualities I already possess in great measure? Is there room for me to improve in certain important leadership traits?" Make your list and resolve today to work on those qualities you want more of. This book provides you with insights and ideas you can use to more effectively bring out your best so you can bring out the best in others so your results will exceed high expectations. You will break your old records, outdo your previous bests and set your own world records.

o   o   o

"The task of the leader is to get his people from where they are to where they have not been. The public does not fully understand the world into which it is going. Leaders must invoke an alchemy of great vision."

Henry Kissinger

o   o   o

Leadership:
If It Is To Be,
It Begins With Me.

The Thinker

Back of the beating hammer
By which the steel is wrought,

Back of the workshop's clamor
The seeker may find the thought;

The thought that is ever master
Of iron and steam and steel,

That rises above disaster
And tramples it under heel!

Might of the roaring boiler,
Force of the engine's thrust,

Strength of the sweating toiler
Greatly in these we trust.

But back of them stands the schemer,
The thinker who drives things through;

Back of the job—the dreamer,
Who's making the dream come true!
                              Berton Braley

>>> 2

Vital Vision

*"I would give all the wealth of the world,
and all the deeds of all the heroes,
for one true vision."*
Henry David Thoreau

Of all the qualities of leadership that are important, perhaps the ability of a leader to create a vision of purpose is the most valuable. A vision is a picture of something that doesn't exist. Webster defines vision as "an imaginative contemplation." It is this compelling, mental image that the leader holds and shares with others to pull the team in a single direction. A compelling vision has an urgency and a magnetism that attracts like a magnet and enthralls the team to follow in a single direction.

A compelling vision, as George Land and Beth Jarman, wrote, "can pull individuals and organizations to their desired futures. The master cellist Pablo Casals was once asked, 'How are you able to play the cello with such magnificence?' He replied, 'I hear it before I play it.' Pole-vaulting champion John Uelses relies on a vivid image of winning to spur his perfor-

mance, and golfer Jack Nicklaus says the vision 'gives me a line
to the cup just as clearly as if it's been tattooed on my brain. With
that feeling all I have to do is swing the clubs and let nature
take its course.'"
    These are all examples of the value of a vital vision. A
vital vision creates a blueprint of the future and it serves as a the
propelling force of creative change. Empowering leaders live
with a powerful vision of the future. The founders of Apple
Computer, Steven Wazniak and Steven Jobs, committed themselves to a remarkable vision: "To change the world by empowering individuals through personal computing technology."
They then demonstrated enormous energy in sharing this vision
throughout their organization, with their customers and within
their communities. Their vision became not only the driving
force of the organization, but the primary criterion by which to
make decisions. Choices are made not just "by the book," refer-
ring to history, tradition, conventional wisdom and conformity,
but by the vision. The vitality of the vision thus takes prece-
dence over the drag effects of past.
    Organizations can harness the power of a vital vision by
following a few principles: Know your vision and purpose,
commit to achieve your vision and purpose, and make our world
a better place by living according to shared values.
    Washington Irving expressed the value of vision when
he observed, "Great minds have purposes; others have wishes."
His insight leads to the realization that without positive
expectancy, we lack purpose. Empowering leaders exhibit this
attitude of expectancy. This shows itself most forcefully in the
way they minimize their losses. They do not grieve over failures
or what might have been. Rather, the leader looks around the
corner in anticipation of the good things that await him. All he
has to do, he believes, is show the determination to get there. He
rejects the notion of 'can't.' As a result he is able to open more

doors than others, strike better deals and attract more energetic and resourceful people to work with him. He sets higher standards and gets others to help him meet them. He wins confidence and nurtures vitality in others. He expects to succeed. When combined with desire, expectancy produces hope. And hope makes all things possible. Living the expectant life is simply an act of good judgment.

Vision is so important to the success of an idea, organization or team that it has been defined by some of the great thinkers of history. Here are a few thoughts about vision composed by people who made a mark on our world:

"Where there is no vision a people perish."
Ralph Waldo Emerson

"You see things and you say 'Why?';
but I dream things that never were and I say 'Why not?'
George Bernard Shaw

"Vision: the art of seeing things invisible."
Jonathan Swift

"No man that does not see visions will ever
realize any high hope or undertake any high enterprise."
Woodrow Wilson

"It is never safe to look into the future with eyes of fear."
Edward H. Harriman

"Great leaders often inspire their followers
to high levels of achievement by showing them
how their work contributes to worthwhile ends."
Warren Bemis

Light Shields

An example of how vision can be shared and improve the outcome of a project was demonstrated when David, a project manager in our Seattle Leadership Development Lab, told us about a problem situation that existed between the sheet metal installer for a mechanical contractor and the rest of the contractors on an important project at the University of Washington.

The sheet metal contractor told David: "The parts I need to shield the lights have not come in and won't be in for 90 days." The sheet metal contractor went on to say, "We can't finish our part of the project; we've done all we can do. We'll just have to wait for three months until the parts come in. Then we can finish up the job."

This dogmatic declaration on the part of the sheet metal contractor put David, the other contractors and the rest of the crew completely out of control. David felt like saying, "I can't believe you. How can you possibly block the whole project? This is just an excuse. You haven't looked for an alternative plan. There has to be another alternative."

Instead, David gave the situation some thought over the weekend. On Monday, he called a meeting of all the contractors on the project.

"We have a problem," he said. David went on to describe the problem(no light shields) in impartial, dispassionate terms then he said: "We're going to finish the project on schedule. Now how can we complete on schedule without the light shields?"

He put the question to everybody on the job who had any impact on the project.

"I would like to meet again with all the subcontractors, the owner and the engineers on Wednesday," David said. Then he turned to the sheetmetal contractor: "I'd like for you to be there and tell us your ideas for solving the problem."

To David's amazement, the sheetmetal contractor showed up Wednesday. And he showed up with a great idea— an idea that would work and would solve the light shield problem. It was an answer to which the sheetmetal contractor was committed, a solution he could implement that would work fine. David got everybody's agreement to buy in. Wednesday's meeting went astoundingly well. The project was completed successfully, and it came in on time.

"The lesson I learned," David said, "is that when I begin with a clear picture, a vision of the desired future and set high standards, remind people of the picture and hold them to the standards and let them come up with their own solutions to problems, they perform in amazing ways."

Leaders don't give up. Leaders don't give in. Leaders set high goals, and they make their vision of the completed project clear to everybody involved. The 21st Century leaders know that to be successful after setting high expectations they have to abandon old ideas about not compromising. They have to find solutions by sharing their vision of the project with the people who have to build it. They know that the people closest to the work have the answers to the challenge of a problem.

The action I call you to is: Make your vision of a successful future clear and do not accept the easy excuses you hear. Ask for the best of everyone you work with. You may be amazed to see performance that exceeds even your highest expectations.

As David pointed out, the vision must paint a picture of the future. Tom Peters, author and excellence consultant, uses different words to express David's ideas: "To be effective, a vision must be crystal clear. While compromise is necessary to build a consensus for action, the best chiefs (in retrospect) are insistent that the main theme not get so enlarged or diluted as to become insipid.

"... Wise honchos know they can accomplish only limited agendas. The number of important problems and opportunities that confront—and distract—leaders at all levels is staggering. The best tack and jib constantly, but, at a deeper level, fight to keep the focus on the main event ..." the achievement of the vision.

Errand Boys

Purpose can be defined as how an individual or organization makes the world a better place. A vision is a compelling image or picture of the purpose having been accomplished. A micro example of what happens when the purpose is missing was given to us by Ken, a superintendent for a major Willamette Valley construction company. He told our Leadership Development Lab the following story:

"I had been treating my foremen like errand boys. I would lay out their work for them, tell them what to do, when to do it, where to do it and even how to do it. I would try to follow up on them to make sure they did it 'right.'

"I thought I had good reasons for treating my foremen like children; I've never had any really good foremen." (One of the hundred or so "good reasons" we have for not delegating and empowering the members of our team).

Ken went on to say: "I realize that, in order to adequately fulfill my responsibilities on a major project I am working on now, it will require hundreds of hours of readying shop drawings. I could no longer work in an overseer role. I realized I had failed to define the ultimate goal of the work to be done. I had failed to give my foremen the benefit of my own vision of the job. How could I expect them to perform proactively with self direction if they weren't clear about the vision of our desired outcome?"

"Lording over" is disempowering and demeaning. Lording over destroys incentive, squelches creativity and most importantly removes responsibility. We are all learning that treating people like robots, discounting their ability to think and make good judgments, and share in the leader's vision, does not lead to improvements in processes, procedure or methods. This micro approach is demeaning and dehumanizing to the person on the receiving end and never allows a superintendent the freedom to explore and find better ways to perform the macro parts of the job.

How about you? Are you willing to let others make mistakes? Are you willing to hold others accountable for desired results, the achievement of the vision, instead of watching every little detail of their job? Delegating for results will truly empower you and others. The payoff for giving people the vision and the power for them to express themselves is an empowered organization.

There's No Indispensible Man

Sometime, when you are feeling important
Sometime when your ego's in bloom
Sometime, when you take it for granted,
You're the best qualified in the room.
Sometime, when you feel that you going
Would leave an unfillable hole,
Just follow this simple instruction
And see how it humbles your soul.
Take a bucket and fill it with water;

Put your hand in it up to the wrist;
Pull it out and the hole that's remaining
Is a measure of how you'll be missed.
You may splash all you please when you enter;
You can stir up the water galore,
But stop, and you'll find in a minute
That it looks quite the same as before.
The moral in this quaint example
Is to do the best that you can.
Be proud of yourself but remember
There's no indispensible man.

Author Unknown

No person is indispensible. The leader who demonstrates vision can expect to leave a part of himself behind. What does this mean? It means that *when you're gone the part of you that will remain is your vision that has been adopted by others to make the unfolding purposes of the organization a reality.*

There are three principles of vision that empowering leaders know and express. They are:

Knowledge of your purpose and vision.

Commitment to achieve your vision and purpose.

Sharing of values to make the world a better place.

George Bernard Shaw believed that true joy in life was "being used for a purpose recognized by yourself as a mighty one; that being thoroughly worn out before you are thrown on the scrap heap; being a force of nature instead of a feverish, selfish little clod of ailments and grievances complaining that the world would not devote itself to making you happy."

Without a compelling purpose, we live life as a fairly haphazard experience, being easily swayed by the latest fad, temporary pressures, or the most recent advice on what others think we ought to be doing with our lives and businesses.

Dust Off Your Dreams

Last night, at the close of a wonderful, full Thanksgiving Day, we began reminiscing, reflecting on our memories of years past. Some fade, a few remain vividly locked in our consciousness. Our 25-year-old niece asked my brother and me for advice on buying a wedding planning service franchise. What do you say to such a question? "You could get let down." "You might lose your $900."

That kind of negative thinking is easy enough. Deana took her degree in Commercial Recreation. She does recreational therapy. She doesn't have experience as a bride consultant. She is outgoing, bubbly, vivacious. She has a good plan for easing into wedding planning part-time. What does she have to lose? A short list. What can she gain? The whole world—her dreams, her vision of herself as successful. And if she misses, if she discovers the franchise really doesn't work or it's not for her, she will have had a learning experience. Isn't that why we're here? And she will have memories—not of what she *could* have done, but what she did.

So, today is the day for you to dust off your old dreams, your visions. Put together a plan. Go for it. succeed or fail, you'll have memories—vivid, technicolor memories. Decide, act, commit, go for it. Just in the planning, just in the deciding, you'll begin to experience a certain lightness. Yes, you'll rise to new heights.

As David and I were driving to lunch yesterday noon, I asked, "How's your real estate portfolio coming?" He announced, "We're closing on our fourth property the 28th of this month." David started investing in real estate about two years ago. Later in the afternoon, Jeff was standing by our office copier when he announced, "We've set a world's record—we closed on our house today." Jeff's been working on that goal sine he was married two years ago.

I've never seen these men more enthusiastic, poised, confident and centered. These events reminded me of James Allen's words in his book, *As A Man Thinketh*: "You are today where your thoughts have brought you, you'll be tomorrow where your thoughts take you, you can't escape the results of your thoughts be they base or beautiful or a mixture of both, you'll gravitate toward that which you secretly most love."

We must impress before we can express. Thoughts, visions held in mind reproduce in kind.

Today, get a clear picture in your mind of the vision your organization or department is committed to. See it, smell it, taste it, hear it. Before you know it, just when the time is right, your vision will appear as the reality of your life. You'll set new world's records, and you'll experience that same confidence, enthusiasm and poise.

Organizations are like people. If they lack a compelling purpose, they cannot help but be uninspired. On the other hand, an empowering leader committed to a forceful vision focuses the energies of the entire organization. Debbie Meier is committed to do nothing less than creating a new system of public education in New York City's Harlem. She took on the daunting task because she truly cares that young people become critical thinkers and creative problem solvers. As superintendent, she insisted on overseeing the entire period of education, from kindergarten through high school, because she knew it required time to build these critical-thinking skills.

Already the results have been impressive. In the first year, a five percent turnover rate in her schools was one-tenth the city wide average. The dropout rate fell dramatically and district-wide test scores improved significantly.

It's pretty obvious that Debbie Meier has a vision and is

willing to follow it with courage, zest and purpose. No one with a compelling purpose and a great vision knows exactly how it will be achieved. Empowering leaders are willing to follow an unknown path, allowing the road to take them where it will. There are guideposts and some rules to follow along the way. Surprise, serendipity, uncertainty and the unexpected are certainly guaranteed to make some changes in our plans to find the future. "Momentum," Max Dupree said, "comes from a clear vision of what the corporation ought to be, from a well thought out strategy to achieve that wisdom, and from carefully conceived and communicated directions and plans which enable everyone to participate and to be publicly accountable in achieving those plans."

Isn't that remarkable? Max Dupree is chairman of Herman Miller, Inc, the furniture maker that was named one of *Fortune Magazine's* ten "best managed" and "innovative" companies. He is saying that values are often thought of as the soft stuff of an organization, something that goes on a bronze plaque in the front corridor. Somehow values cannot get separated from how the business really runs. Because inevitably employees and customers will know it.

Empowering leaders who have vision allow people space, space in the sense of freedom. "Freedom in the sense of enabling our gifts to be exercised," says Max Dupree. "We need to give each other the space to grow, to be ourselves, to exercise our diversity. We need to give each other space so that we may both give and receive such beautiful things as ideas, openness, dignity, joy, healing and inclusion. And in giving each other the gift of space, we need also to offer the gifts of grace and beauty to which each of us is entitled."

Another way to think about the leader's responsibility is to ask this question: What is it without which this institution (yours) would not be what it is? And that is a question you can ask not only of your company but of yourself. What is it without which you would not be what you are? And that of course is *your* vision.

An article in *Training Magazine* refers to a study of vision statements made by highly successful companies, one of them the Oregon company, Nike, the athletic shoe manufacturer. Here is a brief excerpt from the article: "As Nike's example illustrates, corporate vision that galvanize people are not always high-minded statements about the transcendent value of one's products or the spiritual growth of one's employees or the betterment of mankind. But regardless of its tone, a vision must be explicit. Laudable but vague sentiments such as "We believe in service and quality" won't get the job done.

"That kind of soft and fuzzy vision isn't going to inspire anyone. You could take the label off that vague statement and apply it to any company. Twenty years ago, when I first started coaching companies in the creation of vision statements, that might have helped differentiate a company in the marketplace, but now having a vision, values and mission statement has become a standard of corporate behavior.

The article went on to say: "At the other end of the continuum is a corporate vision that fills six three-ring binders and is, in fact, an extraordinarily detailed plan of what the organization should look like in 10 years. Now, how are you going to communicate that vision? That's not a vision, that's an implementation plan. A good rule of thumb is, if it's too heavy to carry around, it's not a vision."

Neither of these extremes fills the bill. I advocate a middle ground whereby a company does these things: articulates its values, decides upon a single driving force that differentiates it in its market, and creates an implementation plan to build around that single point of distinction. You can do this in seven to 10 pages. You can carry it around, yet it must have enough specificity to energize people.

The mission part of an organization's vision is the explicit and concise statement that galvanizes people. When President Kennedy announced in 1961 that NASA's mission would be to land a man on the moon and return him safely to earth within the decade, that was a big, hairy, audacious goal, and a clearly articulated one.

A company may use equally concise organizational shorthand to talk about core values, as in Hewlett-Packard's 'HP Way'. But this makes no sense until after the company has taken the time to define the values it does hold.

Goals Exceeded

Last night, at the conclusion of our Management Team Advance for the top nine managers of a major mass-merchandiser, the director of operations came up to me and said, "I want to tell you how we were able to get a 20-plus percent increase in sales last month."

"I want to know!" I said.

"Well," Duane said, "near the close of the last day of the month, we still had a few hundred thousand dollars to go. One of our store managers began to call around to each of our stores and ask them what their sales were for the day. Then she told the other managers that she was going to stay open an extra 30 minutes. Most of the stores decided to stay open an extra half hour. We sold the additional $300,000 needed and were able to reach our goals."

The chairman of the company then chimed in: "The thing I'm most proud of is that our store managers felt they had the necessary authority and empowerment," he said. "Our store managers felt they were sufficiently empowered to make that decision to stay open an extra 30 minutes without having to check with the operations manager, the president of the company or have a board meeting.

This is a clear example of empowerment, a clear example of the results that can and do occur when we're courageous enough to allow our people the latitude to make the decisions necessary and when we believe enough in them to allow them the authority to make the decisions necessary to achieve the vision.

The company reached its goal of more than a 20-percent increase in sales, which is very important to any retailer these days. It's important for most retailers to demonstrate to their banks, their creditors that they can compete successfully. More importantly from my viewpoint, it's empowering to every member of the team to feel like "I am a member of a winning team," to know that "we did it—we stayed late, and we made it happen!"

What an extraordinary example of the role of the 21st Century leadership—Create a compelling vision, set the sights high, set the goals and then get out of the way. It is the job of empowering leaders to set high goals and create an environment where people feel empowered to do what's necessary to reach those goals.

What about you and your team? What are the roadblocks (real or imagined) that hold your people back, block them from achieving their new records—self esteem-enhancing, empowering world records?

Why not ask your managers supervising team members if they honestly would feel sufficiently empowered to stay open under similar circumstances. If not, why not? Are your store managers given responsibility for profit, held accountable for labor costs, sales value and margin? Then shouldn't they have the authority to make the decisions that can determine sales, profits and costs?

The action I call you to is: Create a compelling vision—a 20 percent increase and then give your managers more authority today! Watch and see if they take the ball. For goodness sake, do not take it back!

If they don't take the ball, do not blame them. Remember, they are acting out of tradition. You may have to dramatize the results you are after to create culture change. Creating an empowered culture is your job. Do it, and you will thrive. Fail, and you take a dive.

Imagine

Yesterday morning, as I sang the Beatles' provocative song, "Imagine," that song from the tumultuous '60s, with its startling lyrics; as I sang along, I thought, "How the world has changed." It is our use of imagination that must proceed all change. And the more revolutionary the change, the more imagineering is required.

Now let's get down to cases. Do you want this week to be the same as last week, or would you like some exciting, progressive, empowering changes in your routine, your results, your relationships and your outcomes? If you're like me, last week's results, routines aren't quite good enough. You want more, better, bigger, easier, faster, smoother. So how can we achieve these results? How can we guarantee that this week will be a breakthrough week, a new paradigm week? Start by stopping. Yes—stopping. Stop all activity, 90 percent of which is habitual, no-brainer. Use your imagination, your brain, for its highest calling: Imagining. Imagine the results you will want to achieve this week. Really see them in your mind's eye; smell them, taste them, really feel them. Haven't you watched the athletes mentally rehearse the high jump, the pitch, the putt?

So, create a picture, a vision, and hold it in your mind.

Thoughts held in mind reproduce in kind. We must impress before we can express. Now, charge your picture with the magnetism of feeling. You'll be drawn toward your new picture, old patterns will fall away, and, when you look back, you'll say, with Neil Armstrong, when he stepped on the moon, "Just like I rehearsed it."

On the following pages you'll find examples of several vision statements. None is presented as an exact or perfect model. You will want to involve your entire team as you develop your vision statement. One of the statements shown is quite famous and was framed more than 200 years ago. It has continued to inspire Americans and other nations. Soon after its framing, the French Revolution occurred. More recently, the reformers of Russia shook the world—inspired by ideas like those expressed in the Constitution of the United States.

You may be surprised when you describe your vision how much clearer your idea of your future will be. All of the companies whose future I've helped to frame with a clear vision statement have experienced a sense of excitement, buoyancy, and confidence. When you create a vision statement, your team will experience the same feelings. The first twenty-one lines of the Declaration of Independence present the will of the people in a vision of their political rights.

"When in the Course of human events, it becomes necessary for one people to dissolve the political bands which have connected them with another, and to assume among the Powers of the earth, the separate and equal station to which the Laws of Nature of Nature's God entitle them, a decent respect to the opinions of mankind requires that they should declare the causes which impel them to the separation.

We hold these truths to be self-evident, that all men are created equal, that they are endowed by their Creator with certain unalienable Rights, that among these are Life, Liberty and the pursuit of Happiness. That to secure these rights, Governments are instituted among Men, deriving their just powers from the consent of the governed—That whenever any Form of Government becomes destructive of these ends, it is the Right of the People to alter or to abolish it, and to institute new Government, laying its foundation on such principles and organizing its powers in such form, as to them shall seem most likely to effect their Safety and Happiness. Prudence, indeed, will dictate that Governments long established should not be changed for light and transient causes; and accordingly all experience hath shown, that mankind are more disposed to suffer, while evils are sufferable, than to right themselves by abolishing the forms to which they are accustomed. But when a long train of abuses and usurpation, pursuing invariable the same Object evinces a design to reduce them under absolute Despotism, it is their right, it is their duty, to throw off such Government, and to provide new Guards for their future security.—Such has been the patient sufferance of these Colonies; and such is now the necessity which constrains them to alter their former Systems of Government."

• • •

Compared to the Declaration of Independence, the following vision statements seem tame, but they are serving their purpose well.

Software Company

"Our purpose is to provide our clients with software programs which will enable them to gain maximum use from their computer investments, with a minimum of adaptation time, and costs; resulting in a higher return on the investment made in the computer, increased productivity and profits for their companies, and to provide our employees with a work environment which is stimulating and motivational. "

• • •

Retail Merchandiser

To provide our customers with merchandise which is up-to-date in style, and quality which is above average. In an environment which is stimulating, courteous, friendly and fun. That adds to the feeling of pride which the customer can take when enjoying the use of the merchandise purchased. To provide our employees with a meaningful fun place to work, which contributes to their personal growth as well as their incomes. To provide our stockholders with an above average return on their investment dollars.

• • •

Financial Services Company

One purpose is to provide our clients with investment alternatives, education and information on how to put money to work, employ professional management, and employ tax-favored investment. To treat our clients with professionalism and dignity. To provide an environment where our key leaders can experience growth, personally, professionally and economically. To create a work environment which will stimulate everyone to work at his highest level.

• • •

Real Estate Firm

To provide an ethical service to homeowners that will enhance the value of their investment in real property. An investment that at any point in time may be utilized as a marketable value that does in fact relate to all economic conditions. This service when satisfactorily performed will produce a profit sufficient to assure the growth, improvement and continuity of the firm and its staff. Contribute to the integrity of real estate as a profession.

• • •

ODOT

The mission of the Oregon Department of Transportation (ODOT) is to exercise statewide leadership and vision in promoting, developing, and managing a statewide network of transportation systems and facilities that: provide efficient movement of commerce and people throughout the state; ensure the safety of transportation system users; enhance Oregon's competitive position in national and international markets.

• • •

Oregon Glass
"The Rite Lite"

An ongoing commitment to develop new and better products that exceed market standards. Provide our customers with quality products, timely and reliably delivered. Involve our employees in a safe and happy workplace with the proper tools and training. Reward honesty, hard work and integrity. Foster an environment that encourages personal growth, leadership and team commitment

"Quality Products By EnLITEned people!"

• • •

Yaquina Bay Bridge Cathodic Protection Project

A partnership dedicated to the restoration and preservation of the architecturally magnificent Yaquina Bay Bridge. This partnership is be based upon mutual respect, honesty, openness, trust and recognition for the fact that all parties take great pride in what they do. In order to ensure enduring pride in this project, all parties are committed to achieving:

• Completion on or before the specified date.
• Maximum cost-effectiveness.
• Enthusiastic acceptance by the community.
• Resolution of disagreements at the lowest possible level.
• A safe workplace resulting in no loss-time injuries.

• • •

Multnomah Kennel Club
Declaration of Customer/Employee
Service Philosophy Vision

We envision an entertainment facility where people from all walks of life enjoy visiting for a matinee or an evening of fun, thrills and excitement. Where guests leave looking forward to returning, and tell others of their enjoyable experience.

Mission

• To provide a quality entertainment experience that is fun and exciting for all guests.
• To provide owners and trainers with an equitable, competitive place to safely run and care for their greyhounds.
• To provide service minded employees with an enjoyable place to work.
• To contribute to the community and state economies.
• To provide our shareholders with an equitable return on their investment.
• To recognize and reward individuals who, by their actions, exemplify the WIN philosophy.

• • •

Benge Construction Vision

Service our customers with accurate and high quality workmanship. Benge's success and reputation are built on the integrity, skill, and pride of our employees. Our company/employee environment encourages growth, leadership, family and a financially secure future. Benge makes the grade.

• • •

Following you will find the heading: Clarifying Vision, Mission, Purpose and Values. The purpose is to help you and your organization clarify what you're doing and why you're doing it. Once you've answered these questions, written out your replies, you may be surprised to learn what you don't know about yourself and your company. This is a good place to start an important inquiry.

Clarifying Vision, Mission, Purpose, and Values

What business are we in?

Why?

Where are we going?

What do we stand for?

Now that you have clarified what business you're in, why, and answered the questions "Where are we going?" and "What do we stand for?" you can consider writing out a Vision Statement. Organizations which are committed to creating an inspired team of empowered players know the value of a vision statement that inspires commitment. Your vision commitment is a description of the aim of your organization. It is the guiding principle that steers the company on a straight path to success.

The Vision

The Vision is a statement of purpose, direction and excellence. This vision does not represent the past, or even the present, it represents a state of excellence to which the team aspires. Therefore, the Vision Statement is a "stretch" beyond current, usual, normal or past performance. Also, the vision reflects the needs of all external and internal customers. Finally, the Vision Statement is created in order to instill a feeling of pride among all team members as it represents their identity.

Vision may be evaluated by the following criteria:

1. Does the Vision Statement include: What you do; Who you serve; Your desired level of quality and efficiency; Issues of responsiveness, professionalism, etc.?
2. Does the Vision accurately represent the hopes and direction of the organization it represents?
3. Is the Vision a permanent, comprehensive statement which reflects the values, culture and environment affecting the organization?
4. Does the Vision affect all of the areas of activity and functions of the organization?
5. Is the Vision Concise, clear and understandable?

If you are going to build an outstanding organization you must build an understanding of the mission which is derived from our common values. This is what makes your organization unique. This mission must be discussed and integrated into individual thinking so completely that people act on it as a team without having to stop and think.

"Great leaders often inspire their followers to high levels of achievement by showing them how their work contributes to worthwhile ends."

Warren Bennis

Practice Page For Creating Your Vision Statement
Paint a picture with words of the future you desire.

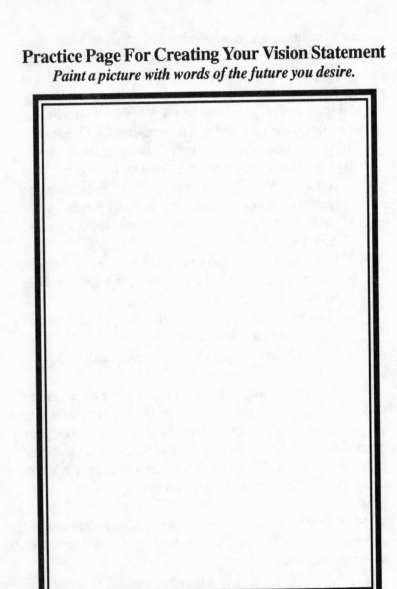

*"All things are created twice,
first in the mind and then in reality."*

It must be remembered that there is nothing more difficult to plan, more doubtful of success, not more dangerous to manage than the creation of a new system.

For the initiator has the enmity of all who would profit by the preservation of the old institution and merely lukewarm defenders in those who would gain by the new one.

Machiavelli
"The Prince" 1513

>>>3

Challenging Change

"Man cannot discover new oceans
unless he has the courage
to lose sight of the shore."
Andre Gide

Gene Faber, the great French naturalist, discovered the perfect example of habitual behavior while studying processionary caterpillars. These unique creatures spend their lives in the forest feeding on pine needles. They move among the trees as part of a long chain with their eyes half closed and their heads butted closely against the caterpillar just ahead of them in a sort of bumper-to-bumper fashion.

Faber wondered, "What would happen if I connected the leader to the last caterpillar in the chain?" Without much trouble, he succeeded in getting a circle going around the rim of a flower pot. Around and around the caterpillars went—for seven days and seven nights. Nothing could break the chain—except exhaustion and weakness from lack of food. And yet food was there in the middle of the pot less than a caterpillar-length away. A feast for everybody if only one of the caterpillars would break the chain, but none of them did. Managers who act like the processionary caterpillars in the new world of change that is confronting us are as outmoded as the rotary telephone.

The Responsibility Of Leaders Is To The Future

Joel Barker, author of *Future Edge,* says the role of leaders in change is inestimable. He was quoted in a question and answer article in *Industry Week* defining how change is affecting human relations in the world of the 1990s.

"It used to be," he said, "that the manager knows the right answer, the workers do not; the engineer knows the right thing, the person on the line does not, and, by the way the boundaries were really clear in terms of who could step where. A worker with a really good idea was usually told to get back in his place. 'What do you mean, you've got an idea for our engineers? You're just a worker!' Well, total quality practitioners completely inverted those rules. What they say now is, 'Our workers are our key people; they probably have the best ideas. Our engineers really should be consultants to our workers.' That's a reversal of rules."

"If you think about it," Barker said, "the responsibility of leaders is almost nowhere in the present. It's about finding the future for their corporation. The key word," he said, " is anticipation. That's what separates the leader and the follower—the leader has the ability to anticipate the future... leaders have to have the willingness to say, 'My God, somebody is messing around with the rules in my business. I'm going to find out what's going on.

"Think of the difference between the pioneer who goes out when things are still at risk (and, by the way, pioneers are always at risk!) versus the settler who's always saying, 'Is it safe out there?' What the settler is asking for is enough data to prove irrefutably that the territory can now be moved into. In the world of 21st Century business, the pioneers will have already taken what they want—leaving for the settler, at best, maybe a commodity market that he can sell to with a trivial profit.

"A leader has to bet. And the bet is that the leader's intuition is active enough, informed enough, perceptive enough that he or she can get the company safely and successfully through the business window of the future. For every company and organization, that will be the bet of the 21st Century. But that's what we're paying today's leaders to do."

Bouncing Back

Kelly told our Leadership Development Lab an inspiring story about betting on his own future.

"It was the first of September, 1978 and I was on top of the world," he said. "I had married my high school sweetheart, I had a good job, and I was making good money. On a Sunday near the end of September my wife left me. On Tuesday of the same week, I came home from work and found the house completely cleaned out—not a stitch of furniture was to be found.

"Approximately three weeks later, the company I was working for went on strike. The friends I worked with (three of the guys comprising half of the crew) decided to strike and the three others crossed the picket line. They all started shouting at one another.

"I hit the street, got another job, looked into school, signed up and went after an education—a two-year degree in electronics. With my two-year degree, I was able to get a good job with a company that is willing to help me by paying for my continuing education."

As I listened to Kelly's story of bouncing back, of literally rebounding from despair, I saw clearly that what happens to us in life doesn't determine the quality of our lives. The quality of our lives is determined by how we respond to these unplanned, unexpected negative changes.

Kelly had all the excuses he needed to lie down and quit. But instead, he drew on his grit. Empowered leaders don't quit. They accept the responsibility for the final outcomes of the events in their lives. They look for ways to overcome problems, not to find "good" excuses for failure. If I have learned anything from the thousands of leaders I have trained in the Leadership Development Lab, it is that we all experience "clipping." We are all knocked to our knees from time to time. The difference between the winners and the "also rans" is that the winners, when knocked to their knees by unexpected, uninvited change, get back on their feet and press on.

The men and women knocking on the door of the 21st Century are beginning to understand that the challenges facing them, more difficult and demanding than ever before, can only be met with a willingness to adapt and change, to follow new paths, blaze new trails and to create new horizons.

Change Inspires Fear

There is no question that significant change inspires fear and although intellect and reason can solve many problems, intellect is generally powerless over fears. Fears are based on emotions and when emotion and intellect cross, emotion always rules. *The Book Of Lists* by Irving Wallace, David Wallechinsky, Amy Wallace and Sylvia Wallace, lists our top fears. According to the list, the number ten fear in our society is the fear of dying. The number one fear is the fear of speaking in front of a group. Most people would rather die than speak in front of an audience. Why? There is nothing intellectual or logical here—this is total emotion.

Reason tells us we need not fear speaking in public. We know there isn't anything to hurt us, but still we quake and our minds go blank. I remember the bank vice president in Peoria, Illinois who stood up in front of our Leadership Lab meeting at the first session and I asked her to tell her name. She looked at me with a blank expression until I pointed at her name tag. She looked at it and told the group her name. You may have had the same experience. Reason says, "I'm not afraid to approach my manager or a complaining customer." Reason says, "I'm not afraid of cold calls or using the phone or asking for referrals." How often does reason lose and fear win? How often do we avoid people and situations out of fear? How often do we avoid change, even small ones, because we fear the consequences? What are the consequences? The negative pictures we have painted in our mind.

Because fears are so powerful and sometimes subtle, we often are unaware of them. This kind of denial—like all forms of denial—is self destructive. Instead of trying to intellectually justify our "not trying" we must honestly admit our fear exists. It takes real honesty and awareness to say, "I'm afraid to compliment people," "I'm afraid to correct people," "I'm afraid of what other people might think of or say about me, they may question my sincerity, my authority." The time you spend working with overcoming your fears will prove extremely rewarding and this project is definitely part of your plan for personal growth, and creating positive change.

Acceptance of change has to be more than lip service. The trick we play on ourselves is that we would like change to happen painlessly, outside of ourselves. We want our spouse to change, our kids to change, our boss to change, our subordinates to change, our neighbors to change. The most important change any one of us can make, and the only change of which we really have full control is our personal change.

Three Approaches To Change

There are three approaches you as a leader can take toward change. One approach is to initiate change, to be one of those who pioneers change, who makes change happen, who breaks through old traditions, old routines, old beliefs, old methods and approaches. Pioneers of change are generally in the minority. They include people like Louis Pasteur, Thomas Edison, Henry Ford and Steve Jobs of Apple computer. And the world is generally better off because of the pioneers of change.

The second approach to change is to cooperate with it. We will go along with change as long as it isn't too new, too difficult, too unusual, too challenging, as long as it doesn't come too fast, too frequently, and as long as it doesn't impact us too personally. We've gone from big cars to little cars and back to big cars again. We've gone from AM radios to FM stereo, from eight track to cassette player to compact discs. For the most part, we all cooperate.

Finally you can resist change. My general experience is that most of us tend to resist the changes which would make the greatest potential contributions, which would give us the most progression because those are the kind of changes that are personal. These kind of changes alter the way we approach confrontive situations. Changes in the way we praise or fail to give praise, changing the way we interact with people we don't relate to, the way we approach the adventuresome, the difficult— these are the kinds of changes we need to make to grow as an empowering leader.

In his book, *The Ordeal Of Change,* Eric Hoffer tells this story of how he reacted to change:

"Back in 1936 I spent a good part of the year picking

peas. I started out early in January in the Imperial Valley and drifted northward, picking peas as they ripened, until I picked the last peas of the season, in June, around Tracy. Then I shifted all the way to Lake County, where for the first time I was going to pick string beans. And I still remember how hesitant I was that first morning as I was about to address myself to the string bean vines. Would I be able to pick string beans? Even the change from peas to string beans had in it elements of fear."

The important question for us is "Why do we resist change?" The answer is that any change that leads to significant growth and progress for us requires us to move outside our comfort zones. How are you like Eric Hoffer? What are the string beans in your life?

Fish Story

For years I wanted an aquarium. One day my wife and I visited an antique store in Seattle, Washington, and I spotted a used aquarium. It was complete in every detail, including an unusual custom-made enclosure cabinet. I admired it. On my birthday a few months later, to my amazement, there it was in my foyer when I walked in the door. My wife had bought it and had it shipped from Seattle to our home in Portland, Oregon. After a few weeks, we set it up in my office with what seemed to be the right fish and accessories, including a little sunken ship with a hole in the side where the fish could swim in and out and hide. One of the fish, which looked a lot like a flat sunfish but a little smaller, always seemed to hide inside the hull of the sunken model ship.

As days and weeks progressed, the fish grew. We commented, "Boy, it better be careful or it's going to get stuck in the little ship." Sure enough, a few weeks later I walked in the office on a Saturday and there it was trying to get out of the hull of the ship, stuck and flapping with all of its might. I reached down into the tank and tried to move the ship so the fish could get free, but it couldn't. It was really stuck. I shook the ship and the fish finally came free. I finished my work in the office, went home, and came back on Monday. To my disappointment, I found the little fish floating dead on the top of the water.

This simple story illustrates what happens to us when we retreat to our comfort zones. We get "stuck" and it can be quite deadly. The walls grow higher, thicker and the chances of escape become less and less. Perhaps it doesn't affect us physically, but in a way more important than our physical bodies, getting stuck affects our self image, our self esteem, and our sense of self-worth. We lose our self-direction. Most of our failures are inside, not outside, our comfort zone. Our real failures occur while standing on the cusp of our comfort zone, peering out and imagining failure. Joe Hernandez, a manager in one of our Labs recently said, "The failure is not in trying—the failure is in not trying." We stand on the cusp, imagine failure, and don't try at all. As a result, we end up as Thoreau said, "living lives of quiet desperation." NBC's *Wide World Of Sports* started its program for years with the slogan, "The thrill of victory and the agony of defeat." Most people know neither one of these enlivening emotions. Instead, they live the lives of quiet desperation which Thoreau described. You have to strap on skis and make the run, take the risk, to ever win the medal. Why do we cling to our comfort zones? We think that by staying inside we obtain security. In truth, real security in life comes from moving out of our comfort zones. Real security comes from experiencing life with all its risks and achieving some measure of success. We can learn inside our comfort zones, but all growth takes place outside our comfort zones.

Jumping Out Of Your Comfort Zone

Kurt, one of our Lab members, was afraid of heights. He set a goal to conquer this fear, to literally step outside of his comfort zone by going sky-diving. So one Saturday, he found himself 4,200 feet up in the sky with the door to the plane open. As the other sky-divers stepped out of the door onto the strut and let go Kurt thought to himself "I'm not going to make it." But he attacked his fear, jumped out of the plane and four seconds later the parachute opened. And then he experience an unprecedented feeling of exhilaration, a sense of power, of having faced and defeated a fear. As the cartoon character Pogo said, "We have met the enemy and it is us."

I'm not saying you need to jump out of an airplane to meet change successfully. I am recommending that you jump out of your comfort zone, run for the nearest comfort zone exit, and you will experience personal exhilaration. Others will be inspired by your example and you will build an inspired team..

Habits, Attitude and Thinking Can Be Changed

We habitually think negatively, fearfully. Have you ever known someone who was afraid of getting sick? What happens? The fear becomes the reality and sickness occurs. Physicians tells us that negative thinking and fear tear down resistance and make us physical and mental wrecks. Worry and stress, forms of fear, weaken our natural immune systems and make us more susceptible to colds, flu and all sorts of illnesses. We can do something about our habitual, negative, self-fulfilling prophecies. Before real progress can take place, we must see those habits and attitudes that need reshaping. Develop the tools to do the job. Watch your strengths become even more powerful and effective as you work through your fears!

How Do We Do This?

1. Understand the comfort zone concept.
2. Think about your fears and inventory a few of them.
3. Address one of those fears—attack it—and watch it disappear. Then address another one. Take little steps; be sure to take action.
4. Inventory your success, your victories, keep track of your achievements in expanding your comfort zone.
5. Celebrate your growth with a trusted supportive friend.

Cliff Jumping

This summer we experienced a record high temperature for the first week of summer. My sons decided that our family should go "cliff jumping," since we are not able to be together much any more. My brother and his wife were with us from out of state and so we all decided to drive to the Wilson River. We arrived at the bridge which spans about 30 feet above the deepest part of the river. My sons jumped into the cold mountain stream. I said, "Well, if they can do it, maybe I can too." As I stood on the edge of the bridge, I was trembling with fear. It was cold and I was scared. I jumped in. When I got out of the cold water I was shivering. I was exhilarated from facing my fear, jumping in and winning. Instead of denying my fear, instead of saying, "Oh, I didn't bring a towel," or "I didn't bring the right clothes," I jumped.

I'm not recommending that you make a decision to jump off cliffs or high bridges into deep, cold streams. I am urging you to jump out of your comfort zone, to address those fears you may have stuffed to the point of not even knowing they exist, and to enjoy the exhilaration that was mine when I crawled out of the water and yelled, "Yahoo! I did it!"

There are only three natural, unlearned fears, as thousands of experiments with babies have shown. "The fear of falling, the fear of closed places and the fear of loud noises." All other fears are learned from vivid experience or from what we have been told by others. The subconscious mind plays a large role in fear. We store reactions to fear in our subconscious mind and they come up and create undesirable situations for us in our daily lives.

The most common fears we have are the ones concerning separation, abandonment and isolation which we associate with change. A child who has been momentarily lost in a department store may retain this as terrifying, emotionally charged fear. Long after the experience has been consciously forgotten, we may have extreme fear reactions to simple situations. We may even find ourselves clinging to the wrong people.

One of the most debilitating fears we carry is the fear that we aren't good enough. When we were children we may have heard from a parent, teacher or peer that "You'll never amount to anything," "You should be seen and not heard," or some equally negative, disempowering, devaluing remark. "Oh, she is a little bashful." "Oh, he is being shy today." As little children, we believe these emotionally wounding, disempowering statements and store them in our subconscious minds.

We learn other fears the same way. We hear our parents or other grownups talk about their fears, their failures, their experiences, their resistance to change. These are all photographed on our minds. We think about them, we wonder about them, we begin preparing the groundwork for our fears. Before we know it, these fears take on meaning, are confirmed in our experience and we have made them our own.

You Can Resolve Your Fears

You can resolve your fears. You can actually overcome them, not by reason but by understanding and action. Fears can make you an extraordinary person. Fears can drive you up and on and be responsible for making you the poised and confident person you wish to become. As you study and experience your fears you will learn to understand them. As you start doing something about them, you will be on your way to a significantly expanded comfort zone, a greater personal fulfillment and you'll be changing your life. You will position yourself to be an empowering leader.

Many people are afraid to take risks. They never learn to swim because they were taught by overly-concerned, well meaning adults to be afraid of water. There are people who are afraid of heights, the dark, crowds, being alone and on and on, all because of an experience they've probably long forgotten. Such fears are inhibiting and prevent us from receiving promotions, achieving our goals and making personal progress. Fears can cause a loss of communications, teamwork, relationships, intimacy, togetherness and happiness unless we do something about them.

You should actually be grateful that you have fears. Every great person who has accomplished much in his life had fears. The great persons have made their fears work for them. How did they do this? They followed a powerful two step plan, the same plan I am suggesting that you follow:

1. They recognized their fears. They identified them. This is the first thing all of us must do. Identify your fears, pinpoint them and make them specific, because that is how you harness the emotion into a positive, progressive direction.

2. They made a plan of action. You will see that only

action dispels fear and turns what could be a liability into an asset. Your plan of action is all important. Remember, "To act is to conquer." To conquer is to bring about change.

Affirmations To Build Self-Confidence

Affirmations are great ways to build self-confidence and to help you welcome change in your life. Here are some practical steps you can take to build self-confidence, further strengthen your self-esteem, and expand your comfort zone:

1. Hold in your mind at all times the self image of good qualities you would like to strengthen.
2. Observe the characteristics of people you admire. Choose a mentor. See yourself as having those char acteristics, qualities and traits.
3. Use these affirmations:
    A. I have strength, power and energy.
    B. I have greatness within me.
    C. I am warm, kind and loving.
4. Meditate on phrases like these:
    A. The life I feel within me is infinite and unlimited.
    B. I love life; life loves me.
5. Use denials to reject attitudes that might cause low self-confidence:
    A. I set aside every negative thought about myself.
    B. I refuse to run myself down.
    C. I reject every feeling of inadequacy or inferiority.
    D. I reject any thoughts of self-pity that creep into my mind.
6. Relabel for self-confidence:

A. Change "I can't" to "I can."

B. Change " I am shy" to "I am interested in others."

C. Change "I am only ..." or "I am just ..." to " I am proud to be ..."

D. When complimented, change "Oh, it's nothing" to "Thank you."

When you conquer a fear or make strides toward expanding your comfort zone, celebrate it with someone who is a friend. Successfully managing change is easier with a friend who supports you and celebrates you. It was Ralph Waldo Emerson who said, "What I need is someone who will help me do the things I can do."

Change is inevitable and constant. You can replace your tendency to fear, resist, and run from change with an attitude of embracing change. By learning how to build your self-confidence, handle your fears, and expand your comfort zone, you can make change happen for you instead of waiting for change to envelope you with a suddenness for which you may not be prepared.

Here are some excuses to avoid. They litter the paths to change and form stumbling blocks if we let them:

Rejection Excuses

Anxiety—I'm afraid I can't do it—Loss of power.

Anger over having your experience made irrelevant by somebody else.

Doubts about the long term success of a new way to do things.

Jealousy because someone is better at the new way than you are.

One of the most important ways to develop change in

yourself is to understand that people demonstrate three common responses to change which leaders should anticipate. They are:

1. People embrace change.
2. People are neutral toward it.
3. People resist it.

Empowering leaders must constantly deal with change and lead others through it. I've identified four appropriate behaviors for managers which make transition or change easier to process. They are:

1. Making change happen.

   This is the behavior that is most supportive of organizational transformation. Empowering leaders take personal responsibility to initiate improvements.

2. Anticipating the need for change.

   Leaders who think futuristically look at the possible effects of environmental change on the organization. They are sensitive to the need for innovation inside the organization.

3. Problem solving.

   This response to organizational change consists of using systematic techniques to make decisions about process improvements. Managers who behave this way look for ways of making change work.

4. Individual alignment.

   The question "What's in it for me; how will it affect me?" is common to all of the responses to change. For people to feel committed to supporting alterations in organizational life, they must feel a personal connection and commitment to changed behavior.

These four sets of behaviors constitute functional responses to change. They are proactive, positive, assertive, and productive. Leaders who consistently engage in these responses actively support change. They immerse themselves in organization improvements and innovation. In other words, they are moving toward change.

The following observation by Theodore Levitt of the Harvard Business School on how to be an effective manager makes it very clear how important the idea of change must be to the leader. "Most managers manage for yesterday's conditions, because yesterday is where they got their experiences and had their successes. But leadership is about tomorrow, not yesterday. Tomorrow concerns what should be done, not what has been done. 'Should' is determined by the external environment— what competitors (old, new and potential) can and might do, the choices this will give customers, the rules constantly being made by governments and other players, demographic changes, advances in generalized knowledge and technology, changing ecology and public sentiments and the like."

And echoing Levitt's observations are these by John McDonald in *Fortune Magazine:* "The business executive is by profession a decision-maker. Uncertainty is his opponent. Overcoming it is his mission. The moment of decision is without a doubt the most critical and creative event in the life of an executive."

Charged Up

The story by Arlen in our Leadership Lab demonstrates what happens when a person decides to change the way he's been doing things.

"I had been taking inventory at our battery distribution center branch for more than a year. I not only did the inventory, I did all the ordering of the replacement batteries. After I completed the inventory and wrote up the orders, I always had to turn my work in to the president (Jim) for his inspection and approval.

"One day, after gathering confidence from my class and

pledging 'never again will I be afraid to stand up, speak out, and be counted,' I called the president of the company at corporate headquarters. We had a 10-15 minute conversation. I told him that I felt I had proven myself, that I wanted all the responsibility and, of course, accountability that appropriately goes with my job, including approving the orders I recommend. I wanted to inspect, be responsible and accountable for all of my work. Since I was closer to our seasonal demands and changing customer base, we would have fewer inventory "outs" and faster inventory turns. This would give us a greater return on investment and greater profits.

"I caught him off guard! He didn't know what to say. He said, 'Let me think about it.' When he called me back the next morning he said, 'It's all yours!' He even went on to say that he wished he had more employees like me—people who would ask for additional responsibility and welcome the accountability that goes with the responsibility.

"I have had this new expanded responsibility and challenge for two months. Everything is going great. I can't wait for review time to roll around."

The lesson I learned is: "When I concentrate on my abilities, take credit for what I have accomplished, all my achievements; it gives me the self-confidence to be assertive.

The action I call you to is: Stay focused on the positive things in your life. Inventory your successes. Write them down. Count them up. Look boldly at your successes. Certainly you have failed, that is how we all learned to walk. We stumble, fall, get up, and start all over again. Take credit for your achievements. Look for opportunities to take on new challenges. The benefit you gain is: You will achieve your goals and get the things you have always wanted. Along the way you will feel changed! Others will get a charge when they look at you; you will be an empowering leader.

It is certainly true that in our century, change seems to be taking us into the uncertain future at a turbo-charged pace, but then consider what John Adams wrote in a letter to James Warren on April 22nd 1776: "All great changes are irksome to the human mind, especially those which are attended with great dangers and uncertain effects."

So decide now—will you wait for change to happen to you—react to circumstances, or will you be proactive, a pioneer of change? Today is the day for you to act. Change some small part of your life and the world for the better and let the results speak for themselves.

o   o   o

So, Change!

Mountains reach up very high,
Sometimes poking through the sky
In mountainous magnificence
But though they tower august, immense
Above me, still they never press
Me down in the heart or make me less;
I wonder if it must not be
Because they know their majesty.
Those who know their worth have no
Need of holding others low,
But secure in their own might
Lift us nearer to their height.
Mountains do not make me small—
When I'm with mountains, I grow tall.

James Dillet Freeman

>>>4

Stand Up For Standards

*"Ideals are like stars; you will not succeed in
touching them with your hands.
But like the seafaring man on the desert of waters,
you choose them as your guides,
and following them you will reach your destiny."*

Carl Schurz

Leaders visualize what they want to accomplish—and how they want to do it. Paradoxically, they lead their teams to share that vision by listening. Leaders acknowledge other viewpoints. They let others inform them while holding on to their fundamental beliefs and principles.

A commercial bank president expressed the value of personal standards in business: "I think integrity is the most practical personal asset a top executive can bring to an organization. You just have to look at the headlines to see the devastating consequences of managerial duplicity or ignorance. When honesty is compromised at the top, an organization can be brought to its knees." If you don't know what you stand for, you will fall for anything. Empowering leaders know what they stand for. Empowering leaders have clarified their values and ideals. They know where they stand on issues like keeping their word and remaining true to ideals that have inspired and anchored them. They know that the single most dangerous thing they can do as a leader is to gain a reputation for over-promising and under-delivering.

One of the most important qualities an empowering leader can possess is integrity. The empowering leader knows that to lead efficiently he must earn and maintain the respect of those he leads. It is many times more important to be respected than it is to be liked, admired, or even loved. The empowering leader is careful about respecting the dignity of others by never saying anything that could be interpreted as hurtful to that person. Empowering leaders have found that they can be tolerant of the views of others, their ideas and even their lifestyles, knowing that tolerance is the first step to achieving respect for and from another person.

All you have to do is to watch the evening news to see what happens when people do not lead from high ideals. We have the examples of Richard Nixon and Watergate, Oliver North and the Iran-Contra scandal, and the insider trading schemes of Ivan Boesky and Michael Milken. These are just a few examples of people who compromised their values. They can teach us to be careful about breaking promises, trusts or commitments. These examples should certainly tell us not to make promises we are unwilling or unable to live up to. If you learn you must break a commitment, communicate it as quickly as possible without blaming others. Empowering leaders have a record of living up to their commitments.

Dr. Melvin Scorcher, author of *Predicting Executive Success,* thinks that companies should ask these kinds of questions when judging the integrity of managers on their team:

Does the individual:

... provide backup to subordinates when they get in a jam, when subordinates take risks that do not pan out?

... recognize and acknowledge personal failings?

... report progress toward objectives and organizational issues truthfully?

... refrain from backbiting behavior when his or her views differ from those of other department heads?

... avoid treating company crises as opportunities to seize managerial power or pin blame on rivals?

Watch to see how people behave under situations that test their personal courage and their commitment. Leaders with high ideals always put the well being of the people reporting to them above their own personal well-being.

Well, how about you? Are you giving your team an example of strong values and high standards that you stand for?

Waiting Waitress

Wednesday afternoon at about two o'clock, I finally got away for lunch. After I sat down in a booth, I heard the waitress visiting with some customers a few booths away. They were discussing another restaurant belonging to the same owners. The customer was saying something about the uniforms being different and the restaurant being a little differently organized. The waitress said, "Yeah, they're having some real problems with management over there. It's a lot closer to my home, but I'd rather drive the extra distance than work over there. I'm hoping they'll get their management problem straightened out, then I'll get a transfer."

Have you ever wondered if managers select their people or if people select their managers? This may be another form of evidence for all of us of how workers really chose their boss—

their manager. I challenge you today to be the kind of leader, the kind of person, the kind of parent, the kind of spouse, the kind of friend that people will seek out, look for, drive an extra distance to be with. By developing the kind of values that attract relationships with others, you'll create the kind of world that people will go an extra distance to be a part of.

Not too long ago I made a cold call on a construction company in Eugene. I didn't know whom to ask for. I didn't know the president's name but a minute later, after approaching the receptionist, I was in his office and as we began to visit I said, "How many key people do you have working here?"

The president got up from his desk walked over and closed the door of his modest office and lit into me.

"All 75 of the people who work here are key people." Once started, he couldn't seem to stop. He told me about buying the company in 1966, assuming all of its debts and paying off every nickel of the indebtedness. It would have been much easier for him to have declared bankruptcy. He told me how easily he made 100 percent more profit on his volume than his competitors do. He said he paid his employees above scale, had pioneered some important technologies, treated every employee uniquely, would not tolerate a trouble-maker, nor a gossip, had zero debt and was committed to truly developing his people. He told me he allows them to fail, has very little turnover, gives appropriate authority and does in fact fire people who will not accept full responsibility, people who are trouble-makers and gossips. Here was a man who demonstrated what high standards can achieve in a company.

You can be an empowering leader like the contractor in Eugene. But in order to gain commitment from employees and associates, in order to inspire them, you must be able to articulate a personal philosophy of leadership—a philosophy that appeals to both the mind and the spirit, a philosophy that is intellectually sound and spiritually inspiring. Leadership philosophy is founded on three important qualities: moral principles or values and beliefs, and high personal standards.

In simple terms, moral principles are the guideposts that help us to differentiate between right and wrong. Empowering leaders must have a clearly defined set of moral principles to which they are committed as the basis for the exercise of leadership. The beliefs of a leader obviously will influence the actions they take. Beliefs are an individual's perception about the realities in the arena in which they operate. In other words, beliefs describe how an individual thinks the system, in their world, operates.

Experiences in real life test an individual's principles and beliefs. As people mature, they must critically evaluate the principles and beliefs that challenge their own standards. As society changes and grows more complex, the empowering leader keeps what is good from the past and applies the quality in those values to the present. Change forces us to reexamine our ideals far more often now days than in other periods of human history. And we regard change that influences us personally, that challenges our values, our concept of the world and our place in it with mixed emotions. The main reason we are unsure has to do with the gaps in the values by which institutions, organizations and businesses operate. These same gaps may be present in the application of personal values to problems as they arise.

The fact is whether a decision to be made is based in the organization or with an individual, it is processed through "personal value filters." The perceptual data that results is actually a projection of our beliefs and value systems onto the decision to be made. The organization that has a strong sense of what is right under any circumstances will not willingly, or energetically, do anything that the members don't understand the value of—or with which their values are in conflict.

When we have to act fast, we don't have time to stop and think things through, we just have to act. So we act from our heart and gut feelings—our spirit and intuition. This is where our values reside.

If the mission of the organization and the values of individuals are not in sync, it is essential to take time to resolve the issues, or individuals and organization end up working against each other. This is why defining values is so important.

When you seek a definition of the values by which your organization will operate, don't confuse what you are going to describe with "vision." Vision is the image of the future. But rather than a fixed point of achievement, values are the ethics by which we make our journey to achievement. Values are the metaphors of the voyage an organization makes to win one goal after another. Values are the golden rule by which the organization can turn liabilities into assets. Values are the practical things such as operating within the law, fair pricing and valuing safety.

A project manager told our Leadership Development Lab:

"Three weeks ago, inspectors from the Washington Safety and Health Administration visited the job site at one of our construction projects. They issued several safety violations because we had not taken adequate precautions relating to fall protection. This inspection came at a time when we were just starting a phase of the work that took place on upper levels in unprotected areas—the kind of work where fall protection needs to be employed.

"Since it is the project superintendent's responsibility to run a safe project, I set up a meeting between myself, the project superintendent and our safety coordinator to resolve the issue and clean up the problems. The project superintendent's initial, defensive response was, 'There's not enough money in the budget for all these safety precautions. Besides, Washington State's rules are unrealistic anyway! We never have to do all that stuff in Oregon!'

"So, I decided to start the meeting using the process of positive correction. I started out by pointing out how well we had been progressing. I reminded all of us how complex the design was and then reminded everyone of the fact that the job was bid at a time when the market was real tight and at that time we really needed the work. Because of this, we'd bid the job extra low.

"I told them that we may not have included enough money in the budget for all the appropriate safety precautions. I then restated our unswerving commitment to safety, and I told the superintendent that we would have a safe project even if we had overruns in this area. I committed to get all the current Washington State regulations to him within the next four days. He committed to me to conform to the standards as prescribed by the state for running a safe and productive project.

"Today we are essentially complete with the work that requires any fall protection, plus we have received several compliments on how safe and clean the project is.

"The lesson I learned is that I can be direct and that the use of positive, professional communication that holds to our values is essential to obtaining the best desired results."

The action I call you to is: Make your standards and expectations clear. Ask for and get a commitment to assure proper accountability to those high standards. Offer help, your commitment and follow-up to your team, and be sure your team does the same. The benefit you will gain is: you will have better working relations and earn the respect of your co-workers. Your team will feel safe and secure and their performance will soar. You will look good to even the most picky inspector, plus your business will earn a great reputation.

Bureaucracy

Our friend, Pete, returned two days ago from his trip to St.Petersburg, Russia (remember, we used to call it Stalingrad, Soviet Union?). He told us about visiting a hospital where they have less supplies than they need for one week's patient care. So much for socialized medicine. He said, "People there wait in lines for hours. If they have enough materials for, say, 50 people, they'll wait until 200 are lined up before they start giving anything to anyone who's in line." This is a bureaucracy—making people wait. Maybe this is the way little people get a sense of power.

Well, how about you—your department, your company? Are you letting people line up, wait with false hopes for an unattainable goal just to tell them, "Later," "It's too late," "No, there's none available," "You'll have to wait a little longer," "Nope, you can't do that?"

The action I call you to is: Don't ask anyone to wait for anything. Give them an answer, now. Remember: Answers for many people, are the supplies they need. By providing people with immediate responses, quality, accurate answers to the questions they're asking—whether it be a friend, your children, a coworker, a customer, a supplier—you'll shorten the line and you'll shorten the cycle-time, you'll build relationships, prove your leadership, prove your reliability. And by shortening lines, you'll break through them.

Clear The Road Blocks

On our way to Eugene, we spotted a capsized three-trailer truck in the north-bound lane. Traffic was backed up for miles, so we were feeling pretty lucky to be going south. We had plenty of time, arrived early, made my presentation to the management team of a major northwest general contractor, jumped in the car, and headed north back to Portland. Beautiful day, things were going extremely well, until we ran into backed-up traffic. The traffic was blocked for miles. We were amazed to discover it was the same three-trailer accident we'd seen four hours earlier—four hours! How could it possibly take four hours to clear the wreckage? Give me four tow trucks and in an hour I'll clear off the wreckage. I have to surmise that there was a lack of determination or a plethora of regulations, red tape, and bureaucracy, or a lack of equipment. And my guess: It was not a lack of equipment. My guess is that it was a lack of commitment, and a plethora of red tape. No excuse, as far as I'm concerned.

Well, how about you? Are you making people wait, holding people up, blocking traffic so the workflow doesn't proceed as smoothly and orderly as it could or should?

The challenge for leaders today is to take a stand for breaking through barriers, breaking through log jams, moving through traffic jams, clearing the way so work can flow smoothly. This kind of smooth flow, this kind of reduction in cycle-time, will help you be in a position to more effectively compete in an environment where customers are demanding faster response time than ever before, shorter cycle-times than ever before. And, while you're eliminating road blocks for others, you'll be eliminating road blocks for yourself.

White Board Manager

I had lunch with Jim, yesterday. It's been over a year since he graduated from our Leadership Development Lab. I'd read in the newspaper about some major shake-ups at his company, so I called to see how he was doing. He said, "Well, I've got a real surprise for you." I said, "What's that?" He told me he'd just been leap-frog promoted from an assistant, to the plant manager position, managing over 85 people. We talked about how different the responsibility is from his formal training as an engineer. We visited about many things. At one point in the conversation he said, "The best manager I ever worked for was in a Hawaiian sugar plant. I've written his name on the white board in my office. No one knows what it means, except me. Every time I look at his name, it reminds me to manage like he did."

I thought to myself, "Wow, I wonder if that Hawaiian manager knows what a difference he made in Jim's life." I wonder if anyone who ever worked for me would hold me up as a model manager. Is there anything more important, more powerful or more meaningful that you and I can do with our lives than to cause others to want to emulate, model themselves after us as the ideal? This leader made a life-changing difference in Jim, and now Jim wants to make a life-changing difference in the people on his team. Each of us has an opportunity to make a real, lasting impact on others. As we assume the mantle of leadership we take the opportunity to change others for the better.

So remember, your job is to do more than build widgets and make a profit. Your job is to build people and make them successful. Your job is to bring out the best in everyone, every person you touch, every person who works with you, so they can realize even more of their potential. By doing this, you'll be realizing your greatest potential.

Your Legends

Tuesday night, at our Portland Leadership Development Lab, I heard two starkly contrasting stories—both of which took place almost 20 years ago. One was about the boss who fired our class member (who, at the time, was the delivery boy), after accusing him of stealing parts from his delivery truck. Our class member learned (later) the real reason he was fired: The boss wanted to give the delivery job to his nephew and didn't have the courage to tell the truth and do the right thing. The second was the story of the boss who loaned our class member $4,000 after his wife left him in the lurch. Here it is, 20 years later, and these stories and the companies are still alive. That's what we call a legend, and legends are what make up cultures. The question for us, today, is: What kinds of stories/legends are we creating? What kinds of stories are people telling about us that will be told over and over and over—maybe for 20 years?

In the end, as we develop new values that permit us to be in harmony with our environment, our professional objectives, our company goals, we have to adapt our values to the crowning principles of our lives. We must put our goals in alignment with our values and they must be in coordination with our inner selves. This was expressed by J. Coudart when he wrote:

"It is rewarding to find someone whom you like, but it is essential to like yourself. It is quickening to recognize that someone is a good and decent human being, but it is indispensible to view yourself as acceptable. It is a delight to discover people who are worthy of respect, admiration and love, but it is vital to believe yourself deserving of these things. For you cannot live in someone else. You cannot find yourself in someone else. You cannot be given a life by someone else. Of all the people you will know in a lifetime, you are the only one you will never leave nor lose. To the question of your life, you are the only answer. To the problems of your life, you are the the only solution."

Up The Pass

Yesterday morning, I took the beautiful drive up the Santiam Pass toward Detroit Lake to meet the young owner of a small construction company. As we talked about his goals, I explained some of the benefits of Leadership Development Lab (confidence, leadership skills, and so on).

He said, "That's what I need. I must develop some of my key people so I can delegate, so I can be running my business and not having it run me."

I was prepared to enroll him in the Leadership Lab, then he said something, "I'm not sure how many of my people I should put in the program."

I was really set back. The program requires a significant investment, and his company is rather small. He only has about 15 people. I aked, "How many people are you thinking of putting in the program?"

He said, "Well, myself, of course, and maybe three or four others."

It was at that moment, when he was the clearest about taking action around his values (developing his key people so he can run his company and not have his company run him) so he could have time with his wife and kids, that his energy began to grow, his face lightened up.

Today, put your words into action. Act consistent with your values. you'll have authentic personal power. Your confidence, self-esteem, enthusiasm will take great leaps upward, and you'll be running your business.

Hosed

The test of personal standards sometimes means that

you have to stand up for what you believe or fail yourself. This was brought home to me by David, who told our Leadership Development Lab: "In the fall of 1973, I was standing on the fantail of a guided missile destroyer outside of San Diego, talking to second-class petty officer, Rubia. We were both looking with interest across the waterway at the dock where some crewmen from another ship were in the process of unloading some fire hoses that we knew had just completed and passed hydrostatic testing. We looked at each other with smiles on our faces because we were thinking the same thing: 'It would sure be nice to have those hoses on our ship.'

"It seemed to us that the chief engineer spent all our budget on the main space repairs, and that there was no money left for accessories like the freshly tested fire hoses we were ogling. Now, there has always been a certain amount of thievery sometimes called 'scrounging') in the Navy. I guess that is a part of the adventure of the Navy—scrounging was really quite commonplace. I said to Rubia: 'Wouldn't it be nice to have those hoses?' and he said, 'Yeah!'

"I went back to my work station and began reassembling a spare pump I needed to finish repairing. About 15 minutes later, I was paged over the general announcing system: 'Report to the chief engineer's stateroom immediately!'

"I arrived at the chief engineer's stateroom as quickly as I could, knocked on his door and announced my report. He invited me in and told me that Rubia had just been apprehended stealing fire hoses from the pier. My heart sank, my pulse increased. He went on to tell me that Rubia would probably go to the captain's mast and then he told me how disappointed he was because Rubia had been such an outstanding leader.

"I can't explain exactly how I felt, but I was very sick to my stomach. I was afraid to say anything, but after what seemed like hours I spoke up. I told the chief engineer that punishing

Rubia was not necessary since I was the one who planted the idea in his head, so I should be the one held accountable for the whole incident. "The chief engineer proceeded to give me the most professional chewing out I have ever received. He even questioned how I could be allowed to wear gold bars on my collar. As it turned out, Rubia was never disciplined.

"The lesson I learned is that honesty and integrity are always the best policies, and that even if there is a tradition of questionable behavior—maybe *especially* if there is a history of questionable behavior—I must lead from high ideals."

"The actions I call you to are: Lead from high ideals. Never compromise your standards. Stand up for standards!

"The benefits you will gain: You will walk about with your head held high every day of your life. You will earn the respect of yourself, and self-respect will lead to the empowering respect and leadership of others."

Appeal To Noble Motives

People have a high regard for themselves and like to be known as fine people. J. Pierpont Morgan said, "A man usually has two reasons for doing a thing—One that sounds good, and a real one. Being idealists at heart, we like to think of the motive that sounds good." So in order to lead people, appeal to their nobler reasons: "You know the right thing to do!" "I can always trust you." "The team is counting on you." "You never let us down." "I appreciate your honesty and integrity." "These are the values of our company. Do you feel in harmony with them?"

> *"Noble be man, helpful and good!*
> *For that alone sets him apart*
> *From every other creature in earth."*

Let your own ideals and values guide you in your appreciation of the ideals and values expressed by others. Often you can provide empowering leadership by appealing to another person's high ideals.

Missing Tools

Dale told our Leadership Development Lab:

"During a period of explosive growth, Bob was requested to help out in a production area. He agreed. Midafternoon, I discovered Bob walking off the job because someone had "stolen" one of his tools. He said he wouldn't work with someone petty enough to steal. I told Bob that we really needed his help and if his square didn't turn up, I would buy him a new one. I asked him to put himself above this petty thief and to please return to the job. The next day Bob came to me and apologized.

"The lesson I learned was the importance of confronting difficult and challenging people issues. At first I was afraid to confront the situation, but by appealing to Bob's high ideals he became willing to pitch in and overcome his childish anger.

"The action I call you to is: to confront the difficult people situations in your life by appealing to the high ideals of your team. The benefit you will gain is: a motivated team of adults."

The Price Of Success

What is the price of success? It means simply to adhere to your personal standards, no matter how tempting it is at times to slide over them.

Success also means using all of your courage to force yourself to concentrate on the problem in hand, to think of it deeply and constantly, to study it from all angles, and to plan.

Success means that you must have a high and sustained determination to put over what you plan to accomplish, not just because circumstances are favorable to its accomplishment, but in spite of all adverse circumstances which may arise. Nothing worthwhile has ever been accomplished without some obstacles overcome.

Success means refusing to believe that there are any circumstances sufficiently strong to defeat you in the accomplishment of your purpose, and it means paying the price of seeing your standards challenged by others.

HARD!! I should say so! That's why so many people never attempt to acquire success. They answer the siren call of the rut, and remain on the beaten paths for beaten persons. Nothing worthwhile has ever been achieved without constant endeavor, some pain, and constant application of the lash of ambition. That's the price of success as I see it.

I believe every person should ask himself: Am I willing to endure the pain of this struggle for the comforts and the rewards and the glory that go with achievement? Or shall I accept the uneasy and inadequate contentment that comes with mediocrity? Am I willing to pay the Price of Success?

You Can't Lie to Yourself

Todd told our LDL class: "In the summer of 1983, I was lead man on a project. We were being paid on an hourly basis for work on a construction site. I was training Fred, a friend of mine in carpentry. Fred wanted to work extra hours, starting his day at three o'clock in the morning. I agreed to let him start before I got there. After a little while, it became apparent that Fred was not accomplishing a lot of work in those early hours. After I confronted Fred a few times, he finally admitted to lying about his hours. He hadn't been putting in extra time and his lie was eating at him. We resolved the situation by working out a payback plan and I decided to let the young trainee save face by not telling the owner about it."

The lesson learned is: "I need to be honest and have integrity in all things." The action I call you to is: "When a situation arises that lends itself to dishonesty—use that situation to prove your honesty and integrity." The benefit you will gain is: "You will have the reputation you deserve."

Four Inches Short

I was impressed when Steven told our Leadership Department Lab a story that demonstrates the importance of standards, even when they can seemingly be ignored without hurting anybody:

"We were installing all the electrical systems for three buildings including the piping for the security system contractor. I assigned Chuck to install all the conduit stubs for security sensors on 17 large power garage doors. After walking through the job site and reviewing the details and the prints with Chuck, I left him to do the work.

"Chuck decided that he could pre-cut and bend the conduit as most of the doors were alike. The next afternoon as I made my rounds, Chuck was almost done except that on about every third door, the conduit was four inches short of where it was supposed to be. When I asked about this, he said he'd made a mistake but was going to cut four-inch pieces to put on top and the strap them on. We walked the job looking at the rest of the work. I complemented him on the rest of his work and told him how professional the job looked. Then I told him I thought that although the four-inch pieces would work, it wouldn't look as professional as the rest of the job. I told him to go ahead and take all the short conduits down and re-cut new ones to the proper length. Chuck agreed and went about his work.

"When he had made the changes and the job was officially complete, I could see how obviously proud of his work Chuck was. Chuck has a clearer understanding of the standard of work expected by our company.

"The lesson I learned is: The importance of going ahead and setting a higher standard than others are used to. Ask it of your team and they will perform to those standards. And take great pride in their work. The action I call you to is: Do not accept sub-standard work out of convenience. Set a high standard of quality. Let quality be the guide for completion. The benefit you will gain is: your employees will perform to the standards you set. You'll gain a quality reputation".

John Luther expressed the value of personal standards in a powerful way: "Good character is more to be praised than outstanding talent. Most talents are, to some extent, a gift. Good character, by contrast, is not given to us. We have to build it piece by piece—by thought, choice, courage and determination."

If you always lead from high ideals you'll never have to reproach yourself for doing something that reduces the regard you have for yourself.

Ben Franklin's Points To Live By

Benjamin Franklin devised 13 points to live by which empowering leaders will find just as valuable as that wise 18th Century leader did.

1. Temperance.

"Eat not to dullness; drink not to elevation."

2. Silence.

"Speak not but what may benefit others or yourself; avoid trifling conversation."

3. Order.

"Let all your things have their places; let each part of your business have its time."

4. Resolution.

"Resolve to perform what you ought; perform with out fail what you resolve."

5. Frugality.

"Make no expense but to do good to others or your self; i.e., waste nothing."

6. Industry.

"Lose no time; be always employed in something useful; cut off all unnecessary actions. "

7. Sincerity.

"Use no hurtful deceit; think innocently and justly, and, if you speak, speak accordingly. "

8. Justice.

"Wrong none by doing injuries, or omitting the benefits that are your duty."

9. Moderation.

"Avoid extremes; forbear resenting injuries so much as you think they deserve. "

10. Cleanliness.
    "Tolerate no uncleanliness in body, clothes or habitation."

11. Tranquillity.
    "Be not disturbed at trifles, or at accidents common or unavoidable."

12. Chastity.
    "Rarely use venery but for health or offspring, never to dullness, weakness, or the injury of your own or another's peace or reputation.

13. Humility.
    Imitate Jesus and Socrates.

o   o   o

Lead From High Ideals
Appeal To Noble Motives

W. Edwards Deming's Fourteen Points

1. Create constancy of purpose for improvement of product and service.
2. Adopt the new philosophy.
3. Cease dependence on inspection to achieve quality.
4. End the practice of awarding business on the basis of price tag alone. Instead, minimize total cost by working with a single supplier.
5. Improve constantly and forever every process for planning, production, and service.
6. Institute training on the job.
7. Adopt and institute leadership.
8. Drive out fear.
9. Break down barriers between staff areas.
10. Eliminate slogans, exhortation, and targets for the work force.
11. Eliminate numerical quotas for the work force and numerical goals for management.
12. Remove barriers that rob people of pride of workmanship. Eliminate the annual rating or merit system.
13. Institute a vigorous program of education and self-improvement for everyone.
14. Put everyone in the company to work to accomplish the transformation.

Total Quality Leadership

"Good, better, best; never let it rest
Till your good is better and your better is best."
Author Unknown

Some people may not know what a Lexus or an Infinite is, but Mercedes Benz knows and so does BMW.

Who is the fourth-largest manufacturer of automobiles in America? Honda!

What happened to Cadillac, Lincoln and Chrysler?

A far more important questions is, "Why?" What do these "foreign-made" products offer that many Americans prefer? The answer is resounding and simple: Quality!

Cadillac may be down, but are they out? "Nobody's putting quality on the road like Cadillac," say current advertisements in newspapers, magazines and on television. Anyone can make a quality claim but Cadillac can back it up. Sales for 1990, a down year for the domestic auto market, went up 12 percent. Cadillac won the 1990 Malcolm Baldrige National Quality Award, the highest award for quality given to a U.S. manufacturer. (Federal Express won the same award in the service organization category and the Wallace Company, a 280-employee maker of pipes, fittings and valves, won it as a small business.)

You might be asking, "What's this got to do with me and my organization? I don't make Cadillacs or Chryslers."

The auto industry story and the Malcolm Baldrige award say that *quality counts*. People will pay for quality. Companies that put quality first not only stay alive, they produce proportionately greater profits.

What are these winners doing that is making a difference in productivity and profits? These winning organizations are implementing an approach called "Total Quality Management" (TQM), which includes the terms, "total quality control," "continuous improvement," "world-class," (JIT) "Just In Time," (SPC) "Statistical Process Control." I prefer to call the approach TQL—Total Quality Leadership.

What effect will TQL have on our lives in the United States?

Leadership expert Tom Peters has said that TQM represents a management revolution in the United States and it addresses the fundamental question confronting Americans in the Nineties and into the 21st Century. That question is, are we willing to accept a permanently lowered standard of living? That's pretty tough language, but it's exactly the language I mean to use. We're at a crossroads in the United States. Seventy percent of our manufacturing industries are now under severe competitive challenge. This is so because we lost our way on the basics—quality, service, and the ability to innovate rapidly. We now need to take bold steps to make a comeback. The time for incremental steps is past. Whether you are small banker, a Mom-and-Pop corner store owner, or a local insurance broker, quality improvement objectives of 100 percent to 500 percent if you are going to survive, let alone thrive.

Thirty years ago, Alfred P. Sloan left General Motors

and the auto industry with this message, "No company ever stops changing. Change will come for better or worse. Each new generation must meet changes in the automotive market, in the general administration of the enterprise and in the involvement of the corporation in the changing world." Today Mr. Sloan's statement not only applies to General Motors and the auto industry, but to all of American industry.

There's something different about change in 1990 as compared to 1980, 1970, 1960 or 1950. And what is that difference? It's the rate of change, the pace of change and the speed at which change is taking place. There's another fundamental difference about the changes that are taking place in our world today. They are as fundamental as those changes which were ushered in by the Industrial Revolution. The harnessing of waterpower in the sixteen hundreds, the invention of the steam engine and the cotton gin forever changed the way we do business. We began to mechanize work so that backbreaking labor could now be done by machine. We began the long road which freed men and women from back breaking toil. The Industrial Revolution ushered in a new kind of prosperity which had never been know in the history of the human race. A new kind of freedom emerged; men no longer had to work from sunup to sundown six or seven days a week. It led to the 40-hour work week. It may have also resulted in our looking at, or thinking about, *people as machines.*

The revolution now taking place may be more difficult to quantify. We are only in the crawling stages of this new revolution. It can be compared to what's taking place in Eastern Europe. We all recognize that a revolution is taking place there, but when did it all begin? Was it when the Berlin Wall fell with the Brandenburg Gate opening in December, 1989, or was it with Lech Walensa's strike in Poland? It's hard to place the date.

But the fact is change is afoot. Exciting things are happening not only in Eastern Europe but here at home.

In American industry, the mother of the revolution is *necessity*. Change is necessary because of our inability to *keep pace* in a world market. For the first time in our present generation, since about 1975, America began to experience a lessening in its standard of living. We discovered that our weekly, monthly and annual salaries bought less. Now, we know that the decrease in our standard of living was directly traceable to our lack of ability to produce quality goods that competed successfully in a global market.

Quality consultant Phil Crosby estimates that presently service companies are sacrificing 40 percent of their sales revenues to poor quality. David Kearns, chairman and CEO of Xerox, believes that "One-fourth of all work in American industry is done to correct errors." Xerox was being eaten alive by Japanese competitors. Then they made the commitment to quality. They developed ways to benchmark against not only the best in their markets, but the best in any market. They slashed suppliers from 5,000 to 300. They decreased defects from eight percent to less than three tenths of one percent. In the end, Xerox reduced costs and increased revenues per employee by 20 percent.

James Harrington, former IBM quality assurance manager, says 25 percent of manufacturing and administrative time is spent reworking defects and errors. In other words, he estimates that eliminating those losses *could increase output by 25 percent without increasing production costs*.

It's conservatively estimated that *one-fourth of all work in America is done to find and correct errors*. Significantly reducing that fraction would allow organizations to increase their productivity without increasing their costs. The key to competitiveness in the 1990s will be an unwavering commitment to *quality improvements*. Conventional wisdom once held that prudent managers shouldn't spend more on improving quality than absolutely necessary. But we have found that the nature of quality is quite different from what was previously assumed. Rather than adding to costs, improving quality lowers costs because total quality holds down or eliminates the cost of finding and fixing mistakes. Only organizations able to meet and exceed customers' expectations will survive and prosper as customers not only demand the highest quality available worldwide, but also expect to pay less for it.

It's taken us some time to realize and recognize that our standard of living is slipping. And some still will not admit it. It has taken us even longer to realize what is the fundamental cause. The *why* of the decrease in quality production and competitiveness has taken much longer to understand. Why has the country that *invented* mass production and provided the highest standard of living in the world for generations *fallen behind?*

There are many examples to illustrate the reasons, although some people may still want to hide their heads in the sand. We invented the VCR machine, but there are *none* made in America. Most of us equate the best television sets, and the best cars with those that are made in some other part of the world. It's statistically true that most Americans would prefer to buy products made somewhere else in the world. Why? Because they perceive the quality to be better. General Motors (GM) finds it difficult to sell its Geo-Metro which is made on the same production line alongside the Suzuki Swift.

Now we're looking hard to see what enabled these other countries, and more specifically Japan, to produce a better quality automobile, a better quality television set, a better quality Walkman. At first we felt it was technology, so we rushed out to invest in robots and more advanced production equipment.

It took seven years and more than $3.5 billion since GM chairman, Roger B. Smith first said Saturn would tackle the very assignment Vega flunked. Smith wanted to prove that GM could build a top-quality small car in the U. S. The car would shame the Japanese? For $1.9 billion, Saturn constructed one of the most highly integrated plants since Henry Ford began building automobiles near the turn of the century. Saturn's facility is able to produce about 240,000 cars a year, including their engines and transmissions. To be profitable Saturn will have to double that capacity. While Saturn was incubating, Honda Motor Co. acted and spent about $2 billion developing its own U.S. car-building operation. Honda developed its facilities in stages, adding capacity as demand required. More sophisticated automation was added as workers became more adept at using it. Saturn, in contrast, attempted to design a facility so automated that it would require few human workers. Honda got started faster. While GM took more than three years to decide that Saturn should have its own plant, Honda expanded its assembly plant and began building its engine factory.

The unfortunate result of GM's strategy is that Honda got not one but *two assembly plants* with total annual capacity of 510,000 cars, more than double Saturn's. Honda also got a factory capable of building almost all the engines, transmissions and related components needed by its auto-assembly operations. The question arises, does GM need an expensive new operation to do what Honda does (build top quality cars) as a matter of course at competitive prices in the U.S.?

To be more competitive than we are was not the result of superior intelligence from the Japanese. They are not significantly ahead of us in most manufacturing sectors in terms of modern manufacturing technology. What we had to finally realize and admit was that the Japanese advantage consisted of *management's willingness to take the responsibility to empower people on the front lines to make decisions that affect operational quality.*

For quite some time, we felt that Japan had a more dedicated workforce. That may have been true. Certainly *it was true* that they had a cheaper workforce; but this is no longer true. Sun Magazine, December 17, 1989, reported that McDonald's in Tokyo was paying $7.15 an hour, while in the U.S. the same job was earning $4.60 an hour. When we watch Honda come to America, build motorcycles and cars in the same towns we're building them, drawing on the same workforce, and building a higher quality product at lower costs with greater profit, we must conclude their secret is not a cultural difference. Their secret is, in fact, a fundamentally different approach of management—an approach to management that could be characterized as revolutionarily different as the changes taking place in Eastern Europe.

Some feel that Gorbachev will go down in history along side Thomas Jefferson and Patrick Henry for his visionary foresight. And Yeltsin will also have his place in history. These two are at the head of the parade that is ushering in something that is so new, so unlike anything the Russian people have ever known before that it takes men of courage, vision, foresight and strength to head the movement.

Like the Gorbachevs and Yeltsins of the world who represent change, we must be willing to embrace new ideas. To be a *world-class competitor, continuous improvement* is going to become an ongoing part of our way of doing business—our way of life.

"Total quality" is the drive to do a thousand things better anywhere and everywhere in your organization. It's the development of deliberate, well-coordinated plans to innovate and excel at everything you do and to strive for perfection continuously. It's a focus on perfecting the process of what is done rather than on calculating how much money is left after deducting the cost of waste, mistakes, turnover, and workplace accidents.

"Total quality" is what's needed to grow and diversify in our competitive global economy. It is within that prescription for how to do business that we're going to find efficiency, effectiveness and value.

There are three ingredients that must be embraced, understood, utilized, accepted, and practiced for Total Quality Leadership (TQL) and continuous improvement to become a way of life. Though these three ingredients are easy to label (Statistical Process Control (SPC), Just In Time (JIT), Total Employee Involvement (TEI)), there must be a commitment that goes deeper than new labels. This new way of doing business *values all employees, values their ideas, values their thinking, values them as persons.* This way of doing business does not project the employee as a cost item on the ledger.

This new way of doing business goes beyond lip service. Frankly, it's so revolutionary that it can't be ushered in with the relative ease of installing a new machine or a new computer. Before we look at how the three ingredients can make a new way of doing business a permanent part of our culture, our business life and our system of doing work, let me give you an example of the deep commitment that I want to communicate.

When the Japanese opened their Nissan truck plant in Smurna, Tennessee, they spent $500 million on equipment, machinery and plant. That's not so surprising. What astounds and amazes us, and what seems to set them apart and makes them unlike most other businesses in America today, is the fact that apart from the $500 million they spent on equipment, they spent $63 million training their employees. That's approximately $15,000 per employee!

Honestly, what is your reaction? How would you feel about spending $15,000 to train some of your employees? Does the thought, "They're not worth it" come up? Do you react,

"Why bother, they're not going to stay here that long anyway?" Do you say, "They'll be retiring soon." Does the idea "Why, what for?" come to mind? I'm sure for some of us it may. This is the fundamental difference, this willingness to *believe in our people, our willingness to commit to our people, our willingness to value our people.*

Since 1980, National Tool and Die increased productivity by 480 percent and pre-tax earnings by 2,400 percent and reduced employee turnover to less than four percent. A case of sophisticated management? No! A simple set of values it practices in everything it does, including teamwork, empowerment, recognition, and absolute respect for its employees.

Visualize a three-legged milk stool. Leg one is "Statistical Process Control;" Leg two is "Just In Time or Materials As Needed;" Leg three is "Total Employee Involvement." I was privileged to hear Dr. W. Edwards Deming recently. Dr. Deming has been referred to as the "Father of the third wave of the Industrial Revolution." General Douglas McArthur took W. Edwards Deming to Japan in 1950 at the end of the second world war. American business wouldn't listen to Dr. Deming. Today Dr. Deming is the person given more credit than any other individual for turning Japan around. The most prized industrial award in the nation of Japan is called the Deming Award for Quality. Dr. Deming brought to the Japanese a concept of management we refer to generally as Statistical Process Control (SPC). In speaking about what's necessary to successfully manage American business Dr. Deming, now approaching 90, said managers must have "profound knowledge." It is this profound knowledge that we can obtain through the appropriate application of SPC. Every company that has made the turnaround to world-class quality has embraced statistical process control.

When Motorola made the decision four years ago to

become a "world-class" competitor, they began down a path which led them to train over 2,000 employees in statistical process control. As a result they earned the Malcolm Baldridge Award, the highest industrial award given in America. When I heard the executive vice president, Bill Smith, speak to over 300 of the top aerospace and electronic managers from Boeing this past January, he was asked the question, "What did the training cost you?" He said,"I have no idea, no way of measuring what the training cost, but I think it cost us a negative $40 million." He went on to say the the actual out-of-pocket costs were about $4.5 million, but he was certain the company had saved at least $50 million.

In the most recent introduction of one of their cellular telephones they experienced a return rate of less than .002 (five out of 250,000 units sold), compared to former models which had a five percent to ten percent return rate within the first 90 days of use. When they introduced this second-generation phone, they enjoyed four times the profit, even though they were in a more competitive, maturing market. Motorola has enjoyed a 24 percent increase in sales without adding any new sales people.

Motorola's suppliers must achieve the same level of perfection and have to apply for the Malcolm Baldridge National Quality Award. We can all take pride in the fact that the Motorola system was accepted as the industry standard by Japan. So, one of the legs in the three-legged stool is Statistical Process Control. It's something we *all* need to know and understand so all managers at all levels can manage with "profound knowledge." Knowledge can no longer be hoarded by a few. Power brokers can no longer be allowed to blackmail the team by hoarding their knowledge.

The second leg on this three-legged stool is "Just In Time," or Material As Needed. Just In Time or Materials As

Needed simply means that we have it *when we need it—in the condition we need it.* This means there is no incoming inspection or hoarding, there is no stockpiling, there is no warehousing, there's no "Just In Case" inventory. It also means there is no waiting. It means we have it *when we need it,* where we need it, as we need it, in the shape and form we need it. It means we do not run our department, our plant, our division, our operation, our line, our area of business on the basis of having more than we need because we're afraid we won't be able to get what we want when we need it. It means that when we do need it, it shows up in a perfect form at the time we need it in the place we need it, with predictable certainty.

Partnering with suppliers is required to make "Just In Time" (JIT) function as desired. Supplies are reduced to the minimum. The hourly workers who produce the supply visit the hourly workers who use the parts. If defective supply is received on the line, an hourly worker calls the top executive of the supply company, day or night, at home or office, to find out what can be done to correct the problem. It means that every employee, in all work groups begins to think of functional teams with which they coordinate as customers. It means that we deliver to our customer what they need, in the form they need it, and with a high degree of professionalism. Walt Disney and McDonald's are excellent examples of such service companies with consistent products and fast, friendly service.

Parked

If we earn the reputation of "crying wolf," we will never get the cooperation we need from our suppliers. Chet told one of our Leadership Labs about a general contractor who called his paving firm on Friday and said, "We have to have you there on Monday to pave the parking lot." Chet knew better. Over the weekend he did an on-site check. Chet and his crew arrived on Tuesday only to discover that the lot still wasn't ready for paving. The next time Chet will wait even longer—be late two or three days. How can we expect to run an efficient, productive, profitable operation if we cry wolf and ask for more than we need, before we need it?

On a very hot Thursday afternoon, I arrived for an appointment with a client who manufactures camper-trailers in central Washington. The general manager kept me waiting for over thirty minutes (not his style or mine). When he finally came out to greet me he looked harried, apologized profusely and began to tell me his story. "We ran out of glue last night. We had to send the night shift home. We still haven't been able to get enough of the right kind of glue for our guns. It is going crazy around here. Let's get together next week." These are two perfect examples of the high cost of over or under estimating the time supplies are needed.

The third leg of the stool is Total Employee Involvement. This means that everyone is empowered and accepts the responsibility for continuous improvement. Making it faster and making it *better* must go hand in hand. Better means fewer errors, less scrap, fewer accidents, *less costs and less waste.* Total Employee Involvement means we value every person. Decisions are pushed down to the lowest possible level. Ideas are sought for and received from people up and down the line. People are listened to and respected. We recognize that two heads *are* better than one. This is not a meaningless cliché. This new way of doing business says the people who *know the most* about the work are the people who are closest to the work, and the people who are closest to the work are the people who can figure out ways to improve quality, efficiency and effectiveness. This philosophy takes the position that people do want to do a *good job,* people do want to do *good work,* and if *asked, listened to, and rewarded,* they will perform *superior work in a superior way.* Employees at Maryland Bank National Association feel so good about themselves and the jobs they do, that seventy percent of new hires are referred by existing employees.

One fact we know for certain is that the companies which have succeeded in truly moving into the Nineties and becoming world-class are embracing continuous improvement, have not done it easily. We have learned it *can be done.* We have learned it will not be done with one meeting, with one bulletin, with one policy statement or with a slogan or banner alone. It will not be done overnight. It will take time. The effort must be consistent. We may fall back, and there will be those who are entrenched in their old ways of doing business. It will take great courage on the part of those who *will persist.* Some of those who will champion this "continuous improvement process" will be at levels within the organization where we have not expected leadership to emerge.

If we've learned anything it's that *All Excellence Comes From Volunteers.* You can't make people give you their best. You can't make people give you their heart, their creativity, their ingenuity or innovativeness, but you can be an example of what it takes to master Total Quality Leadership.

What is involved for the average company to get started with the philosophy of Total Quality Leadership? I've answered this question in part in the foregoing, but now let's look at some specific ideas. Here are eight of them:

Quality Leadership

The key word is "quality." It means providing customers, owners, project managers and architects with performance that exceeds their expectations.

To provide such quality, you, as highly skilled managers, must know what quality is and what your customers' expectations are.

TQL is both a philosophy and a set of management techniques. It includes:

1. Making a commitment at the highest levels stating that quality is the organization's top priority—even before profit. You take this stand because you believe in your gut and know from experience that survival and profitability depend on quality.

2. Clearly identifying who your customers are. It is not as obvious as you might think. Every person who receives an output of your work is a customer, including suppliers, inspectors, owners, architects, supervisors and co-workers.

3. Focusing on preventing service (or production) problems before they occur—instead of finding and fixing problems or defects once they have occurred.

4. Systematically collecting data to guide decision-making, and making that data available to everyone who can use it, especially those actually doing the work. This includes measuring customer satisfaction. (This becomes profound knowledge).

5. Involving everyone in the organization, at every level, in problem-solving, planning and error-prevention. You do this because those doing the work know best why the work is or is not going well. (TEI—Total Employee Involvement).

6. Improving work flow between departments by solving communication problems, conflicting priorities and other jurisdictional issues. "That's not my job" is no longer acceptable. Quality is everyone's job. (JIT—Just in Time).

7. Constantly training and retraining employees at every level.

8. Making "continuous improvement of products and services" the norm for your organization, not just a one-time effort.

What about the customer? How do we define the customer under TQL?

The Customer

A customer is anyone, outside or inside your organization, to whom your organization or any employee in it provides products and services.

That is a different definition than most of us use. We tend to think of the customer as the person or organization that pays for what we deliver.

Under this new definition, anyone you provide service to is a customer. If you are the boss, your estimators and foremen provide you with products and services. Therefore, they need to know what you view as quality. "What does excellence look like?"

Also, just as you are their customer, they are your customer. You need to provide them with quality products and services including: The best in delegation, problem-solving, materials, tools and management systems to get the job done.

Customers typically think of quality in terms of attractive or beneficial product and service features. They also view quality as freedom from trouble, or service that treats customers as human beings with ideas, concerns and feelings—not as adversaries.

You must find ways to determine if all your customers (those who pay you and those you pay) would rate you as providing quality service.

Before you can provide such quality, you need to know

two things:
- • How you as an organization define quality, and
- • What your customers mean by quality.

Common Sense

You may be saying, "What I'm reading is just good common business sense. So what?"

How much good sense do you actually and systematically implement in your organization? Everyone likes to think that their organization is continuously improving. You probably are already doing some things that are part of a TQL program. Have you been doing them long enough to quantify and track improved quality productivity and profitability? Providing quality takes long-term commitment and persistence.

Do you feel some of these ideas are unrealistic and impractical? Where does that attitude lead? It gets most organizations stuck in a "there's-no-way-way-to-solve-that-problem" rut, which makes you more vulnerable during economic down turns. Organizations using TQL effectively have moved beyond "Yes, but ..." to "What if ...?"

Customizing TQL

In a small organization, it may seem like these changes would take resources you don't have and cannot afford. The truth is, the smaller you are the more easily you can manage changes in the way systems work and people behave. In some ways, it is easier to lead a squad than it is to lead a regiment.

Your personal attitude and example play a much larger part in the success of TQL, and while it may be hard to change personally, your changes do not cost much in terms of money or other material resources. Ultimately, the successful implemen-

tation of TQL depends on:
- Your will.
- Your long-term goals and commitments.
- Your energy and skills as a leader.
- Your resources.

Start by choosing one problem that is solvable, or one improvement that is within reach, and solve it, improve it.

Next, ask yourself how you could make things even better—continuous improvement. Use that experience as a model for tackling the next problem or opportunity.

There is a lot of evidence that proves how motivated and collaborative employees and customers become when they keep hearing the message, **"Quality Matters."**

When your workers and customers believe that you want to improve, and that you want ideas from them on how to improve quality, they usually respond enthusiastically.

Costs and Benefits

TQL is not cheap. Time to think, to plan, to implement, to train, to buy the tools—all of this costs money. Where does the money come from, especially in tight times?

Research and your own experience indicate that people at work spend approximately 25 percent of their work year not working. Instead, they spend it taking vacation, on holidays, using personal leave days, taking breaks, doing personal things, arriving late, leaving early, taking long lunches, waiting for supplies to arrive, daydreaming, talking and so forth.

Research shows that people spend about 35 percent of their time actually doing the work—that is, doing work that matters, working on the right things, working in the right order, working at the right speed, producing at the right time and doing it right the first time.

People spend up to 40 percent of their time redoing work—making mistakes, finding them, fixing them, finding out what to do next, dealing with customer complaints, inspecting, being inspected, responding to interruptions, redesigning work and working on the wrong thing.

That is where our lost dollars are. It's also where you can most easily recapture needed dollars, pay for quality improvements and increase your profits.

You have more control over this cost than almost any other. Take any contract project or production line you are working on right now and multiply the cost by 40 percent. Think what you could do if you had that money.

If you are saying, "Our organization is well-managed, we don't lose 40 percent redoing work," then take any reasonable percentage (be honest with yourself) and multiply out the savings. This is your opportunity to make work more meaningful, fun and profitable.

Better yet, collect data on how much poor quality (scrap rejects, inspections, excess inventories) actually costs your company.

You may be shocked. Shock often leads to the impulse to hammer on employees, to force them to do better. Instead, involve them and your customers in identifying where and why the rework is occurring and then figure out ways to reduce those defects to zero.

Be a student. No boss can know everything. Having reduced rework substantially, ask yourself again (and include your customers), "What can we do to add quality to our product and service?"

"There is an infinite difference between a little wrong and just right, between fairly good and the best, between mediocrity and superiority."

Orison Swett Marden

o   o   o

Increase Innovation
Improve Employee Morale
Increase Organizational Flexibility And Responsiveness
Improve Productivity
Enhance Reputation
Increase Profits

"When Spider webs unite,
They can tie up a lion."
Ethiopian Proverb

"A single arrow is easily broken,
But not ten in a bundle."
Japanese Proverb

"One man may hit the mark,
Another blunder;
But heed not these distinctions.
Only from the alliance of the one,
Working with and through the other,
Are great things born."
Saint-Exupery

>>> 6

Synergistic Teamwork

"It is better to focus on results.
This means that you as a leader
articulate vision and values regarding quality.
You develop individuals and teams,
and you reinforce small achievements."
Author Unknown

Not too long ago Roger, who was attending our Team Management Program as a part of an eighteen-month Quality Improvement Program we conducted for his firm, said, "Larry, you have ruined *Star Trek* for me." He went on to explain:

"Several weeks ago I was relaxing, watching my favorite TV show, *Star Trek—The Next Generation.* I noticed that the characters were behaving in a manner that has taken all of the detached enjoyment out of the program for me. They were clustering in circles. The officers of the starship *Enterprise* were sitting around, working and talking, in circles just like the circles General Motors borrowed from the Japanese and used in their Saturn project. The goal was to improve quality by using a team approach to work processes.

"The Turbo Management System program at Smurfit Newsprint opened my eyes to the changes I saw in *Star Trek— The Next Generation*. The training sessions taught the value and need for a consensus approach to decision making, including the correct way and reason for conducting performance team meetings. We even learned that the arrangement of the room is important. The preferred arrangement, we learned, is in a circle, or is a semicircle facing a flip chart. I noticed that when the crew of the new *Enterprise* is faced with a problem Captain Picard calls everyone to the Ready Room, and his officers sit facing each other at a table in a circle. Everyone is invited to air their view of the problem and its causes, and to make suggestions for solving the problem and meeting the challenge. On the bridge of the new *Enterprise* action assignments are made and the command team sits in a horseshoe-shaped sort of sofa, facing the main view screen.

"The seating arrangement to be avoided in a team meeting is the traditional one of a group clustered around, or arrayed in front of and below the leader—the old Captain Kirk style. This is probably what set me up for the realization that there has been a fundamental change in the management style of the United Federation Of Planets. The actual trigger was Larry's comment which compared the old style of management to Captain Horatio Hornblower, C.S. Forrester's fictional character who sailed the seas at a time when long distance communication was nonexistent, and except for a handful of officers the crews were pressed into service. Navy ships were out of touch with civilization for months and even years at a time and had only nebulous goals and objectives. Decisions could only be made by the captain who commanded the ship with a lash— who could literally make a crewman walk the plank. A bit of little known trivia is that Gene Roddenberry, the creator of *Star Trek*, as a youngster idolized Captain Hornblower and later used him as the model for the role of Captain James T. Kirk.

"Now on Saturday evening instead of sitting back and enjoying *Star Trek,* old and new, I find myself picking them apart. Here's Captain Kirk, perched on his throne at the center of the bridge, the classic old style boss from the Fifties confronted with a problem. He calls in Mr. Spock and Bones and makes a vain attempt at a consultive decision making before going ahead and doing it his own way (command decision making), charging off and leading the team himself and nearly getting killed in the process because it is 'his job.'

"An hour later I'll be cringing while Jean Luc Picard, ever the efficient 25th Century manager, agonizes over some situation ably supported by Data, Number One, Facilitator Troy, Dr. Beverly, her son Wesley, and Kunta Kinte. Eventually they'll probably decide to beam Worf down to the planet for some intelligence if the aliens haven't already died of boredom. At the end everybody will have adjourned to Ten-Forward (Whoopi's place) to celebrate another small success in the conquest of outer space."

Command To Commitment

There is a difference in management styles of the modern 21st Century manager and his counterpart 25 years ago. Because we have discovered that team management is a method of tapping innovative ideas of those closest to the work—a way of moving from command to commitment. Team management results in more effective processes, produces continuous improvement and creates empowered employees. And the difference is apparent even in TV dramas like *Star Trek.* In the quarter of a century since *Star Trek* began the move from command decision making to a consensus team approach, the role of management has changed remarkably.

How about you? Are you contributing to an empowered team that is included in all decisions that affect their work and lives and that plays full out each day?

Golden Scraper

Team satisfaction directly impacts the quality and the productivity of the team. This was demonstrated to me while we were conducting a Team Management training program for a Portland asphalt paving company. Sam, the foreman said: "When I had my team meeting with our front line paving crew, I told them we were having a few problems with density of the paving material. When I explained our standards and goals, it gave the crew an overview of the project. Their response was that they didn't know about the density problems. Once they were included in the picture their attitude was, "We can make a difference and it sure feels good to be included, not just rolling asphalt."

Sam presented his best operator from the previous week with his *Golden Scraper* award. Everybody loved it. Of course, the *esprit de corps* went up, production went up and so did pride in their work. The crew, equipped with pertinent information, solved the density problem.

As I listened to Sam's report, the lesson I learned, once again, is the importance of including everyone who is part of the landscape in the big picture and never asking anyone to do anything unless you've sketched the big picture for everyone by telling them why they are doing what they are doing, and what outcome you are looking for. Include your team in the big picture and the benefit you'll gain is an extraordinary increase in quality production, profit and pride. This pride will help you and your team smooth over difficult problems.

Here are the key attitudes empowering leaders encouraged among team members:

I make a difference here. I know that what I do makes it possible for my office to run smoothly. The effort I put into my job shows up in the quality of my company's services, in my company's earnings, and eventually in my own paycheck. I'm part of what outsiders see when they judge my organization. With every letter, every phone conversation, every personal contact, I make a statement about the calibre of service we offer. In the course of a year, I make hundreds of valuable business contacts for us.

How I present my face to the world affects the people I work with. I help to set the tone. I know that when I am enthusiastic on the job, I make a contribution few others can equal.

I shoulder the responsibility for what bothers me. When a situation is causing me trouble at work, I approach it as my problem. Whether it's a procedure that isn't working, a practice I feel is unfair, or a person I am having difficulty working with, I do what I can to change the situation. Sometimes it takes patience. More often than not it requires knowing when to speak up and when to wait and how to use my powers of persuasion with rationality and coolness. When I can't get a situation changed, I look for ways to minimize its effect on me. Most important, I remember that I have chosen to work here, and as long as I'm here I'll give my best.

I take an interest in my company. I know that our organization is greater than the sum of its parts and has a life and personality of its own. I'm interested in how this company got to be what it is today, how people in it have grown as it has, and how my knowledge of the workings of the company not only helps me in my work, makes the work more interesting, makes me a valuable employee, and it helps me set my own career goals and plan my future.

Horsing Around

The fact that an organization is greater than the sum of its parts was demonstrated for me in an unforgettable way by a story I heard of a contest in the Canadian woods. It was a contest to see whose horse could pull the greatest amount of weight. All the local citizens were excited and the festivities were going strong. Most of them were wagering on their favorite horse. They were bragging, speculating, sizing up and calculating. When all the dust cleared, the winning horse pulled slightly more than 9,000 pounds. The one that came in second pulled only a little less than 9,000 pounds. Then, in the post-contest excitement someone asked the question: "How much do you suppose both those horses could pull together?"

Heads snapped, eyes sparkled and after a sufficient amount of calculating, bets were put down again. Most of the bets were about 18,000 pounds as the maximum load the horses in tandem could pull together.

The horses were hooked together and then they gave a mighty pull. And together they pulled and they pulled (why don't you take a second right now and write down the number of pounds you think they might have pulled?) and they pulled some more. When their load was measured, they had pulled thirty thousand pounds! They proved that with teamwork when you achieve synergism, nine plus nine equals 30. Synergism comes from the Greek and means to work together—literally means the whole is greater than the sum of its parts.

We all want to be partners. We all want to be part of the winning team. To make a team, we must be willing to embrace change, be open, vulnerable, but most of all we must be willing to earn and give trust. Today grant others the opportunity to be partners with you by earning and granting trust and you'll experience synergism and it will lift you to unbelievable heights.

Crew Team

Jim, a heating and air conditioning contractor in Seattle told our Leadership Lab that while he was in college he was on the crew team. He said that when the crew team was pulling in unison, synchronized, the boat would literally rise from the water. It almost skimmed across Lake Union. Jim said that for the crew to lose the synergetic effect of that extraordinary teamwork, only one team member had to be out of pace. For the boat to get that lift, all team members had to pull on the oars with the same amount of stress at the same time.

One crew member pulling early or one pulling too late can make the difference in any endeavor. Through training the team members learn to pull with the same amount of stress and to have the coordination to speed up at the right pace. It is the coxswain's job to call out the cadence so that they know how and when to pull. The empowering leader provides the same guidance as the coxswain.

Uncle Bill

When my uncle Bill came home from World War II, he took his mustering out pay and bought a farm near the center of the United States, in Carter County, Southeastern Missouri— red clay country, the foot hills of the Ozarks. My uncle had been in the South Pacific, had been in Hawaii and the Philippines and you may wonder why he bought a farm in the middle of the United States after he had seen paradise. Of course, the answer is pretty obvious. He went home, back to his roots, back to where he had grown up.

In 1946, there was something you could not buy which was a central tool to farming. And that farm implement was a tractor. Not being able to buy a tractor, my uncle did what my Grandad had done before him. He bought a team of mares, and began to plow with those mares. I was there one noon when he came in for lunch, and my Aunt Ruth was cooking on the wood-burning stove. I think what he said was profane, that's why it stuck in my mind. I was very young at the time. But I do remember clearly what he said to my Aunt Ruth, "When I go back out there this afternoon, I'm going to put Bess in the barn, and I'm going to make Mabel do all the plowing." Why? You wonder? Because it was his opinion that Bess had been doing all the straining on the harnesses during the morning plowing and Mabel had just been walking along at the side. He was attempting to do some training. I know nothing about training horses, but I know something about human beings. There are a few humans who are called self-actualized people, and these self-actualized people—almost like saints—will rise above resistance and perform at extraordinary levels regardless of the support they receive. These are rare individuals. Most of us let up if we feel let down.

It's the job of the empowering leader to create a culture in which all the members of a team feel supported, and as a result no one feels let down, no one lets up, and everyone pulls their weight equally at the right time, in the right manner, heading in the right direction, resulting in the magic of synergism.

Sister Sharon

Ford Motor Company has slashed its labor costs by improving the number of cars produced by workers each day. It takes Ford just three workers per car per day to build a unit according to a report by Farbor and Associates, a respected independent research firm that studies manufacturing. Chrysler Corporation ranks second in productivity using just under four workers a vehicle. General Motors continues to lag in the productivity race using almost five workers per vehicle. All these auto makers have improved productivity, but they still have a long way to go.

This study caught my attention because I grew up down the street from what we referred to in my Michigan town as "The Ford Plant" and I remember very distinctly the feelings of the workers at the Ford plant which I would characterize as less than enthusiastic, though more people worked at the Ford plant than any other single employer in my little town. I can honestly say I never talked to anyone who enjoyed working at this Ford plant. This is in stark contrast to my recent conversation with my sister-in-law, who has been a production worker at Ford for over 17 years doing a job quite similar to the one her mother did for more than 30 years. Sharon told me with excitement about Ford's new management philosophy. Team Management she called it. She said that the foremen are no longer going to be the "bosses." She was really excited about that because she's felt harassed at times in the past by her foremen. The foremen's new role is to serve as coaches and mentors, people who are available as a resource person instead of a person who is there as a task master making sure the workers are doing what they are supposed to do when they are supposed to do it.

Well, from Ford's results it looks like the team philosophy is working. The executives at General Motors are saying they hope to "Saturnize" the General Motors organization because of the success of the Saturn. Saturn's success has resulted from the robot mechanization of the plant and the empowered team approach.

How about you? What are you doing to involve your people, to ensure that they have a voice in the decisions that affect the quality of the work they perform? If you still think that Team Management is a fad, think again. If you haven't figured out how to do it, join General Motors and many other firms who continue to fall behind. One thing I'm increasingly sure of is that those companies which fail to find a way to successfully implement a team approach to management will be those whose names will fade from the "In Business" to the "Used To Be In Business" list along with Hannah Car Wash, Pay-N-Pak, Studebaker, Schwinn, and Sears; though it is not out of business, I was shocked to hear that it closed down its catalogue operation at the same time many new catalogue sales companies are prospering.

Empowering Teams Through Consensus

The way to develop self-managing teams is to make them autonomous through delegation and training. Don't just dump responsibility on them and set them up to fail. Train, train, train. This means that you migrate to a different type of control. Managers have control leaders have influence. You lead through using quality technology on the tasks that need to be done to actualize your vision. If your people follow, you have influence.

When you autonomize your team, you can expect some "dumb" decisions. Don't leave them alone. Work actively with your people, help them to test their ideas and learn from the process. Move your people from being a group to being a synergistic team that uses quality technology in all of their decisions and plans. Participatory-decision-making is relatively easy; implementation of the decision can be tough.

A winning team is a team that more than ordinarily comes alive when each member really appreciates the transcending power of unification into a group. Remember two horses can pull more than three times the load of each one individually. Following is one prescription for a winning team. It came to me in the form of an ad I discovered for a company called Signode Industries, Inc. It appeared in *Business Week Magazine*.

How To Build A Winning Team

For the good team, each member holds the same vision.

The crew members want to be right where they are. They understand the risks, as well as the rewards. They know when difficulties present themselves, they must pull together.

The more experienced are willing to set the pace and lead by example.

But the great team?

You sense a unique harmony when the oars touch the water. The oarsmen carry a penetrating sense of purpose. There is an unspoken confidence. It is as if only this group, right now, is doing the task exactly this way, with a special rhythm and commitment.

Making The Team Concept Work

Who should be on the team? is a question that often creates confusion. The answer is everyone who answers directly to that manager or everyone who is part of a functional group. Anyone else? If any team members have an assistant or lead person (backup), it would be logical to invite that person to those meeting in which that person's area is being discussed. Ideally, team member and team leaders have backups to represent them in the event of illness, travel, or other cause of absence. In fact, if there is no designated number two person, it might be desirable to use team members (on a rotating basis) for this purpose. It may be that the team leader's team leader should attend occasionally for specific purposes: to give recognition for achievement, to help identify a problem and ask for suggested corrective action. Peers of the team leader may benefit from and contribute to some meetings, also. Ideally, every team leader should attend every other team leader's meetings. Realistically, because of time constraints, this seldom happens unless there are inter-departmental matters to discuss.

Meeting Objectives

Once company and departmental team goals have been determined and committed to, supportive individual goals should be negotiated and action steps determined (with performance timetables). Each team member should experience empowerment by concentrating on critical areas for results. (A critical area is one which can contribute to profits such as saving time, improving quality, shortening cycle time, reducing rework, improving functionality, enhancing customer satisfaction and reducing costs.) The team leader may have a better perspective in this area than the team member, but, assuming that responsibilities have been clearly defined, consider asking team members to determine the most vital goals to be achieved within a given time period. If the team members have demonstrated their managerial perspective in agreement with the team leader's goals and they have emotional ownership of the goals, then chances of goal achievement will be improved. Meaningful goals are derived from accurate measurement of prior performance.

Remember that one major purpose of setting goals, baselines for performance is for team members to succeed. Goals must be measurable. For example: "To increase sales" is not a goal. But to increase sales 20 percent over the previous quarter is a concrete goal and a time period should be set to accomplish the goal. If sales last month were at an all-time high and this month is traditionally a slow month, you may want to negotiate this goal downward. Actually, this exchange indicates a need on the part of the goal-setter for a little education in the purpose and process of goal-setting. Perhaps a better goal in this instance would be to achieve a percentage increase in sales over the same month last year.

Some strategies are offered as goals, and that may be acceptable. For example: "I'm going to become a better motivational leader." How will you know when you're making progress in this area? Productivity (or sales, or quality) will improve. Now all you have to do is determine realistic amounts and set a time limit and you'll have a measurable, quantitative goal, i.e., to increase productivity 10 percent over last year as an example. Being a better motivator may be an appropriate strategy to achieve this goal.

Goals must be completely controllable by the goal-setter. If the achievement of the goal depends in part upon someone else or another department, individual responsibilities and timetables must be clearly defined and established. If you establish a shipping date for a customer, you are dependent upon production as well as shipping to meet that goal. Related departments must coordinate in setting goals if they are to achieve them.

State goals as results. Adding a new person to the department is an action. Why do you want to add the new person? To free others to be more productive? To improve the receivables record? To reduce rejects? What results are you after? Ask questions to arrive at goals fitting these criteria.

Reviewing Goals

Once goals are established, the empowered team reviews them frequently enough to avoid frustration (if they prove to be unrealistic, they will be adjusted downward) and to avoid inaction (if they are accomplished in less than the allotted time, they will be negotiated upward). Remember, achievement of maximum results and continuous improvement is your over-all goal. Use the team meeting to compare what has actually happened with the goal. Appropriate recognition is given to goal achievers; help is given to those who fall short of their goals. Even if there are no other items on the agenda, this alone is productive use of team members' time.

The Meeting

Holding the meeting: Distribute an agenda well in advance of the meeting to insure preparation and to get team members' input as to items that should be added. Empowering leaders know that goal achievement is extremely important to the team and every member on it. The empowering team leader meets regularly (at least monthly). It works better if this is a regular time—fourth Thursday of the month, first work day after the third. Effective team leaders get broad and active par-ticipation from their team members. This allows them to take minutes themselves, using this outline:

Action Decision	Who	When
Achieve sales of $125,000 with a gross profit of 30% ($37,500).	Hiram	3/31
Ship orders of $125,000 on schedule	Zeke	3/31
Reduce rejects to .5%	Myron	3/31

Or an outline of your own preference that includes the above elements.

Empowered Team Members
Are Ready To Share Responsibility

High performance team members share responsibilities and it makes things run much smoother. As an example I showed up on a Saturday morning early for a meeting at a Beaverton hotel. I was disappointed to find that the meeting room wasn't set up correctly for the workshop. I called catering. The person who answered seemed confused about my request. Housekeeping was near by so I walked over and asked for what I needed which was clearly outside of housekeeping's normal area of service responsibility. Their response, "Let's see what we can find." They found what I needed and I got the meeting room set up the way I wanted it. Everything went smoothly and the event was extremely successful. All of us must be willing to share one another's responsibilities if we are to have a winning team. If one person doesn't cover their base another person has got to cover it for them if we are to have an empowered team. And when we do cover for each other the customer gets what they need. It's a winning, empowering experience for the customer. Don't be afraid to ask for the authority you need. Make certain that you cover your position and that you cover the positions of others when you are asked, and ask for what you need to do it. The benefit you will gain is a sense of personal empowerment. Individual empowerment leads to team empowerment. You'll have successful events and a personal sense of achievement.

Following are four excellent reminders that will help you maintain better team cooperation. They are the Teamwork Checklist, Coaching Hints for Team Members, the Team Meeting and the Motivation Checklist.

Teamwork Checklist

1. Maintain open communication lines.

What are sources of essential information? Who needs to have that information both within and outside the performance team? What is the procedure for distributing that information? Are ideas encouraged from all employees?

2. Keep team and overall company plan current.

Are team members involved in the development and updating of plan's? Of performance? Are all committed to the plan? Is it challenging yet realistic? Do team members accept direction? Are all aware of the importance of controlling inventory? Of meeting production schedules? Improving quality? Reducing overtime?

3. Provide stimulating leadership.

What motivates individual team members? (Each is unique.) Are all familiar with team performance and overall company goals? Does each person understand the importance of their job and how it relates to the accomplishment of these goals? Are all trying to improve?

4. Develop a clearly defined organizational structure.

Are all areas of responsibility goal oriented, clearly defined and assigned? With no overlapping and no voids? Are these definitions reviewed and revised as necessary? Does the leader delegate effectively? Is time recognized as a precious resource?

5. Create and maintain a current procedures manual.

Were all involved in development of procedures? Do the procedures contribute to productivity? Part of new employee training? Do team members accept and abide by established procedures?

6. Sustain a feeling of mutual respect among team members.

Do team members have career plans? Is there a "driving" spirit evident in the team? Do all strive for excellence? Do some occasionally settle for "good enough?" Is there a strong feeling of interdependence both intra- and inter-departmental?

7. Give recognition for achievement.

Is improvement encouraged with positive comments? Do team leader and team members alike recognize goal achievements? Is praise undiluted? Mechanical or spontaneous?

As we are increasingly more effective in the above areas, we'll generate an "our-company-against-the-world" feeling to replace any internal bickering.

Coaching Team Members

1. Set the example:
   A. Establish high personal standards.
   B. Expect Team Members to do the same; provide guidance.
   C. Understand that Team Leaders "set the pace."
   D. Create a company-team concept.

2. Negotiate Team Members' goals:
   A. Establish and mutually accept business goals.
   B. Encourage and support personal growth goals as well as business goals.
   C. Be sure that Team Members have emotional ownership of goals.

3. Expect Team Members to recognize and correct their errors:
    A. Provide counsel in using strengths to overcome weaknesses.
    B. Guide and encourage independence.
    C. Be sure that ground rules are mutually understood.

4. Be supportive with Team Members:
    A. Listen to team members during regular one on one contact.
    B. Empathize with and encourage them.
    C. Be available for advice in implementing their action programs.
    D. Keep them informed as to how they're doing.

5. Measure progress and maintain improvement awareness:
    A. Compare performance against goals regularly, weekly or monthly.
    B. Interpret goal achievement in terms of contribution to profit and achievement of overall mission of organization.
    C. Recognize successful performance.
    D. Maintain continuity and momentum in goal-setting/achieving process.

The Team Meeting

1. Formation of team:
    A. Employees who answer directly to you.
    B. Others who should or need to attend.
    C. Establish procedures and objective and get agreement.

2. Meeting procedure:
   A. Compare performance against goals by posting progress on performance graph.
   B. Review "goals-in-progress."
   C. Team consultation on corrective action.
   D. Get Team input—tap their resources.
   E. Negotiate new goals.
   F. Discuss matters affecting goal achievement.
   G. Discuss policies and procedures (if appropriate).

3. Holding the meeting:
   A. Distribute agenda well in advance.
   B. Meet regularly (preferably weekly).
   C. Define/re-define responsibilities.
   D. Follow steps in #2 above.
   E. Keep written record of goals and action steps and any other important decisions.

4. Pitfalls to avoid:
   A. Absenteeism.
   B. Unrealistic goals.
   C. Starting later.
   D. Running overtime.
   E. Indecisiveness.
   F. No time limits.

Motivation Checklist

Jon R. Katzenbach and Douglas K. Smith coauthors of *The Wisdom of Teams: Creating the High-Performance Organization*, described how to build team performance in an article for "Harvard Business Review:"

"Although there is no guaranteed how-to recipe for building team performance, we observed a number of approaches shared by many successful teams.

"*Establish urgency, demanding performance standards, and direction.* All team members need to believe the team has urgent and worthwhile purposes, and they want to know what the expectations are. Indeed, the more urgent and meaningful the rationale, the more likely it is that the team will live up to its performance potential, as was the case for a customer-service team that was told that further growth for the entire company would be impossible without major improvements in that area. Teams work best in a compelling context. That is why companies with strong performance ethics usually form teams readily.

"*Select members for skill and skill potential, not personality.* No team succeeds without all the skills needed to meet its purpose and performance goals. Yet most teams figure out the skills they will need after they are formed. The wise manager will choose people both for their existing skills and their potential to improve existing skills and learn new ones.

"*Pay particular attention to first meetings and actions.* Initial impressions always mean a great deal. When potential teams first gather, everyone monitors the signals given by others to confirm, suspend, or dispel assumptions and concerns. They pay particular attention to those in authority: the team leader and any executives who set up, oversee, or otherwise influence the team. And, as always, what such leaders do is more important than what they say. If a senior executive leaves the team kickoff to take a phone call ten minutes after the session has begun and he never returns, people get the message.

"*Set some clear rules of behavior.* All effective teams develop rules of conduct at the outset to help them achieve their purpose and performance goals. The most critical initial rules pertain to attendance (no interruptions to take phone calls), discussion (no sacred cows), confidentiality (the only things to leave this room are what we agree on), analytic approach (facts are friendly), end-product orientation (everyone gets assignments and does them), constructive confrontation (no finger pointing), and, often the most important, contributions (everyone does real work).

"*Set and seize upon a few immediate performance-oriented tasks and goals.* Most effective teams trace their advancement to key performance-oriented events. Such events can be set in motion by immediately establishing a few challenging goals that can be reached early on. There is no such thing as a real team without performance results, so the sooner such results occur, the sooner the team congeals.

"*Challenge the group regularly with fresh facts and information.* New information causes a team to redefine and enrich its understanding of the performance challenge, thereby helping the team shape a common purpose, set clearer goals, and improve its common approach. A plant quality improvement team knew the cost of poor quality was high, but it wasn't until they researched the different types of defects and put a price tag on each one that they knew where to go next. Conversely, teams err when they assume that all the information needed exists in the collective experience and knowledge of their members."

Decision-Making At Lowest Levels Of Work

Plugged In

Well, I finally did it. I plugged in my own personal computer. With some assistance from one of my associates, I turned on one of our office computers and began to play around with it a little bit. It was time to go home (there were only two of us left in the office), and I asked John, "How do you turn this thing off?" He said, "Well, I turn it off at the power plug."

Of course, there is an on/off button more conveniently located on the back of the computer. I said, "Why the power plug?"

He said, "Because if you wear out the switch on the back of the computer it is much more expensive to replace than the one on the power cord."

I didn't know how much more expensive it is to replace the computer switch than to replace the power plug or how soon a computer switch is expected to wear our. This computer I was playing with was four years old and the switch seemed to be holding up fine. I am certainly not going to get down on my hands and knees to turn off the power plug each time I am ready to turn the computer off.

John's values and behaviors in this situation, however, are powerful examples for me of the extreme importance of pushing the responsibility for costs and the authority for decision making to the level closest to the work. This is called "empowerment." And it means that the work group responsible for the output is accountable for costs and has the authority to make the decisions that affect costs.

In empowered organizations, people are constantly looking for ways to cut costs, improve efficiency and eliminate waste—right down to turning off the switch that's the least expensive one to replace.

As an empowering leader in your organization, a part of your responsibility is to find ways that empower people to make cost-saving decisions. One of the important ways you can do this is by developing a recognition system that singles out those who have made suggestions—given you ideas—that are cost cutting, money saving, quality improving or cycle shortening.

In addition to recognition, it is important to reward in tangible ways those who do help you to cut costs and improve efficiency. The ability to enlist the eager involvement of your team helps you qualify as an empowering leader. This kind of empowering leadership will help you maintain your market edge, help you enrich the lives of each member of your team, build moral, decrease turnover and win in a world that is increasingly competitive.

Lead The Way, Or Others Will Lead You

As I was enjoying my winter vacation with our kids in California, I took the opportunity to pore over more newspapers and magazines than I normally read in months.

I read this headline in one: "GM's Resistance To Key Trends Puts It Behind." In the mid '70s, Toyota was followed by other Japanese automakers who found a way to prevent the annoyance of having to carry an extra key and fumble around to look for the right key for the ignition of your car. Toyota came up with a single key for all locks, and which is insertable in either direction—one key that unlocked the ignition, door, trunk and glove compartment.

More than 20 years after the single key was first introduced, General Motors has yet to adopt the idea and, as far as anyone knows, is not even considering the simplified customer-friendly single key—in spite of the fact that research shows customers much prefer a single reversible key.

GM continues to issue one key that operates the doors and trunk and a separate key for the ignition. Only GM's Saturn brand (which accounts for 6 percent of the 3 million cars GM sells in the United States each year and operates autonomously from its parent) has switched to one single key.

This isn't the first time GM has resisted innovation. The

automaker was behind the pack in bringing out advanced engines and transmissions. GM also fought against seat belts in the 1950s and air bags in the 1980s, maybe explaining why the world's largest corporation lost billions last year. It seems GM ignores the customer's viewpoint.

The path to superior customer service, true competitiveness, and remaining in business to the year 2000 and beyond—remember, there are no guarantees—is "Listen to our customers, really listen, set the trend, set the pace, don't resist any innovation or improvement."

Jack Welch, who was dubbed by Fortune magazine as our leading change master, made several observations in his book *Control Your Destiny Or Someone Else Will.* Among them:

"I've made my share of mistakes—plenty of them—but my biggest mistake by far was not moving faster."

I wonder how GM feels about the quote as it applies to keys, seat belts and air bags. More importantly, how about you? What innovations have your competitors set the pace on?

"The three most important things you need to measure ... are customer satisfaction, employee satisfaction, and cash flow."

My experience is that most of us are far better at measuring cash flow, more committed to it than we are at measuring customer satisfaction. After all, customer satisfaction is harder, less tangible, more difficult to gauge. The very idea of feeling that we are supposed to satisfy employees is a new idea for many of us. I thought the employee was supposed to satisfy us. something to ponder!

"Any company that's trying to play in the 1990s has got to find a way to engage the mind of every single employee. I'm sure as I've been about anything this is the right road. If you're not thinking about making every person more valuable, you

don't have a chance."

Making every person more valuable is the whole idea behind team work. When a team works well together, results are much better. A general contractor asked Walt, the president of a Seattle excavation company, "How can you afford to send all of your people through Turbo Management System's training?" Walt replied, "How can I afford not to?"

How about you? Do you take the leadership role in innovation and change, or do you wait for others to lead the way? Worse yet, do you resist the obvious trends? Or worst of all, do you ignore customer feedback about performance, telling them that you really know best what is right for them?

o   o   o

Pulling Together

The Leader's Prayer

Dear Lord, please help me—
To accept human beings as they are—
    not yearn for perfect creatures;
To recognize ability—
    and encourage it;
To understand shortcomings—
    and make allowances for them;
To work patently for improvement—
    and not expect too much too quickly.
To appreciate what people do right—
    not just criticize what they do wrong;
To be slow to anger and hard to discourage
To have the hide of an elephant
    and the patience of Job;
In short, Lord, please help me be a better
leader.

Adapted from John Luther.

$$>>>7$$

Show Genuine Interest

"Every man's affairs, however little,
Are Important to himself."
Samuel Johnson

A genuine liking for and a sincere interest in others results in personal charisma and magnetism. By developing the habit of caring for and about others like you care about yourself, you can become a dynamic, empowering leader. Oprah Winfrey, the fourteenth highest-paid entertainer in America, says that one of her business secrets is to "treat people the way you want to be treated." You strengthen your ability to lead only when you have shown genuine interest in the people you work with. Take a personal interest in the welfare of your subordinates. Ralph Waldo Emerson said,"It is one of the most beautiful compensations of this life that no man can sincerely try to help another without helping himself."

Unconditional Love

At about noon, on Saturday, a new friend of ours

stopped by our house—a lovely young lady. We could see she'd been crying. Our natural response was, "What's the matter, honey?" She said, "I just came by to tell you guys how much I love you. You're the only people who have ever loved me unconditionally for who I am, not for what I do, achieve or accomplish."

We decided long ago that love for family and real friends is non-negotiable. We may not, and often don't, approve of every thing our kids do or have done, but our love is non-negotiable.

Today would be a great day for you to communicate to those you love that your love for them is unconditional, not dependent upon the way they look, the way they dress, their grades, or their achievements. It is unconditional. This will free you, and it will free them to be the best that they can be.

Know Your Clients

Recently, I conducted the first session of our 10-week sales training program for a sales engineering firm here in the Portland, Oregon area. Let me give you a little background. A week before the program started, we toured a plant serviced by our new client. In other words, we found out where our new client sells their services, what they sell first-hand, to whom it is sold, and what the customers like and dislike about our new client's products and services. So, when I conducted this training session, on Monday morning, I drew on 25 years experience as a sales trainer. But in some ways, far more importantly, I drew on my awareness about my client that I developed by touring their customer's plant. I led from a base of conviction about "what we do, how we do it, and how it applies " to the real world of my new client.

The lesson I learned, once again, is the importance of

getting to know—really know—my clients, listening to them, knowing them, knowing their world. Take the time to get to know your customers better, your clients—internal and external. The benefits you'll gain are: renewed confidence and enthusiasm. Clients have every right to expect a supplier to learn their business.

Guess what happens when a sales person is not attentive? The following anecdote demonstrates the consequences:

Yesterday, Clifton and I made an important call on a new client—the sales manager of a local firm. He told us about a call he had received from a client who asked that the sales representative assigned to this account be replaced. Why did the client "fire" the sales representative?

The answer was that this sales person had not shown any real interest in the client's business. "She doesn't understand our business and seems unable or unwilling to learn about our products and our customers' applications."

The client had gone so far as to invent code names for its products just to make it easier for the account representative to remember the product names and applications. Still, she could not (or would not) remember. It seemed to the client as though she really didn't care about them, their business or their products.

I have heard complaints for many years that some sales people are self-centered, care only about "the sale" and are indifferent toward the client. Others complain because some sales people don't really *understand* the client and the client's world.

The situation I have just described is one of the most blatant examples of self-centered complacency I have ever heard.

As you might have guessed, this particular representative was subsequently removed from the account. To say the least, this was quite a career setback for her. To her credit, she admitted that the customer was right. She vowed to commit herself to all future accounts to get to know the clients, their business and why and how her client's products or services are important.

One of the fundamental leadership principles utilized by empowering leaders in their pursuit of excellence is "Become *Genuinely* Interested In Others."

"Kindness is irresistible, be it but sincere and no mock smile or mask assumed. For what can the most unconscionable of men do to thee if thou persist in being kindly to him?"
Marcus Aurelius

The action I call you to is: Redouble your commitment to all of your customers (both your internal and your external customers). Commit to knowing their needs, understanding their problems and truly helping them solve those problems. The benefits you will gain are strong client relationships, smoother operations and career advancement. You will be an empowered and empowering leader.

Toward Intimacy

We recently rented the much-acclaimed movie, "The Doctor"—a story based on a true experience of a physician who treats his patients (and, as it turns out, everyone else in his life) like objects. His rationale: If you get too close to your patients, you'll lose your objectivity and therefore your effectiveness. When he is diagnosed with throat cancer and goes through the indignities and the abuses of being a patient himself, through the ordeal of chemotherapy and surgery, he discovers that he really lacks intimacy with everyone in his life, including his wife and son.

As I watched this movie it came to me that we all desire intimacy and that many of us may be looking (as the song says) "in all the wrong places." The only way we can find the joy of intimacy is through risk and vulnerability. The paradox is that through the loss of our defenses, we find ourselves. We find our true identities. Today would be a great day to drop any defenses, to risk intimacy, to run the risk of letting down and letting go of the persona you present to the world. Let your true individuality show through. By doing this, you'll experience a deep connection with those you love. And, through this connection with others, you'll experience extraordinary power as an empowering leader.

A Kinder, Gentler Return

I stopped by Meridian Park Hospital yesterday afternoon, to see Clifton. Clifton had spinal surgery yesterday morning. They literally slit his throat to go in and replace the disk at the base of his neck. There he was, tubes in both arms and tubes in his neck, yet he was up, optimistic, forward-looking. Clifton knows full well that he will change some of his dramatic, dynamic life-style for the foreseeable future—a man who has made more than 1,500 skydives, has run in more than 30 marathons, and does 40 sit-ups, push-ups and leg-raises, every morning. At one point he said, "Boy, this has gotten me in touch, this has gotten me grounded again. I know I'm surrounded by many loving friends." My natural response was, "Clifton Pieters, you're getting back exactly what you give out so freely. I've never known anyone who is a more caring, sensitive, giving person than you are."

Practice a kinder, gentler approach with those you love, today. The benefit you'll gain: You'll experience the same kind of feedback, the same kind of returns—kinder, gentler returns—

from those you love. And you'll receive the support you need at the time and in the place you need it most.

Reach Out

Following through on an intuition, I called a long-time friend in Phoenix. "How are you doing, Judy?" She responded, "Oh, I was thinking about you—it's really hectic here. I've sure been busy and things are kind of up and down."

I said, "What's up?"

"Oh, Marlin passed out at work the other day (Marlin is a marketing manager of National Fruit company's office in Phoenix). His office called *me*. I asked them why they hadn't called 911 and gotten him to the hospital. I jumped in the car and rushed over to his office. By the time I got there, he had been revived. He said it was just indigestion. I insisted that he go the the hospital. Well, he had a mild heart attack."

Judy was very macho through this whole story until she said, "His boss, who is in California, never did call us. He has our home phone number; he could have called us." Her voice broke. I supported her the best I could.

I was glad I followed through on my intuition and reached out to a person who was hurting, even when I didn't know exactly what to say. Follow your hunches and you will prove to yourself that they are often more reliable than your brain. Reach out to everyone in your world, especially at work, even when you don't know what to say. Be willing to be vulnerable. The benefit you'll gain is a greater sense of personal pride and self-respect, and you will help build an empowered championship team.

To be an empowering leader you can't work with everyone in the same way. People must be treated in the light of their character, position, and personality. By showing them that you know who they are, and that you respect them, you demonstrate interest. Make full use of the small points you know about the people you work with. Show them you know how they feel, what matters to them and what pulls the plug to their enthusiasm. Mirror the behavior, mannerisms, style, gestures and actions of the other person. This is especially important when talking on the telephone. If they speak slowly, slow down. If they speak quickly, speed up. Adjust yourself to their pace, their style.

Talent Scout

Phil told our Seattle Leadership Development Lab that he had a new fellow on his job he hadn't taken the time to get to know, and he wanted to employ some of the ideas from the Leadership Lab and intuitively knew (as we all do) that the better we know a person, the more effectively we can work together. So, he took the time to do what we call an "inner-view." He began by asking the new man questions to try to get acquainted and really get to know him. To Phil's astonishment, the new crew member had been a foreman on similar jobs in the past. At one time he even owned his own construction business. Phil told our class that this fellow had a lot of great ideas that could improve the project. Phil said he never would have found out about the ideas or this person's talent and ability if he hadn't taken a few minutes to just get to know him. How about you? Who do you need to get to know better? Become a talent scout today: Go out and conduct your own inner-views.

You People

Early one morning during the pre-election contest for the Presidency, I was surprised to hear that Ross Perot had withdrawn. Why? No doubt there were many reasons. High on the list of conclusions about his withdrawal was that he wasn't prepared for the process. This was demonstrated by his *faux pas* in front of the NAACP audience. He referred to his audience as "you people." After a heckler corrected him he apologized and less than five minutes later he said it again, "you people." He seemed to have so much going for him. He was leading in all of the polls and ahead of both of the other candidates. And then his *faux pas.* He lost his opportunity.

Once again, I was reminded that we can have technical skills, technical knowledge, we can have all of the knowledge we need, we can be highly motivated and enthusiastic, but, if we lack the people skills needed—if we offend or turn people off— we lose our opportunities. In this section of *Empowering Leadership,* you will find ways to strengthen your people skills. As you find ways to strengthen your human relations skills, you'll be strengthening your leadership skills. The benefit you'll gain is the full value from all of your other qualifications and knowledge, and you'll break through as an empowering leader.

Lunch Break

Red, a project superintendent, told our Leadership Development Lab, a marvelous story about himself and one of the key people he coordinates with in his office. Each of them has a different style. They work together and it's important for them to work well together. Red's a little more deliberate, a little slower in making decisions and may appear indecisive. She's quicker, maybe a little impulsive. Red was determined to improve their relationship, so he took her out to lunch and asked about her interests, successes and goals. As it turned out, they had a lot more in common than either of them realized. When it came time, recently, to hire a new receptionist, Red had his ideas, and she had hers. Red listened to her ideas, and the new receptionist they hired is great. Red has made it a point to brag to everyone about *her* decision. Red said, "It's much easier to have a winning team when you take and express an interest—a genuine interest—in all your players."

The action I call you to is: Find a way, today, to express your interest in and for every member of your team. You'll build relationships and gain cooperation.

During his second term in office, Theodore Roosevelt was asked to reveal his secret of dealing successfully with all kinds of people. He replied, "I never judge a man until I discover what he would *like to be* as well as what he is." Taking a genuine interest in others enables us to find out what they want to be or would like to be. And, the knowledge of what their desires, motivations, ambitions and ideals are, put us in a far better position to work with others successfully, to lead others successfully, to bring out the best so results exceed high expectations.

Notice and remember the other person's wishes and preferences in small matters. You'll make a deep impression and win both their friendship and confidence when you demonstrate that you have them in mind, by reflecting their behavior and style. Discover what people really want, especially the exact nature of their most active desires which touch upon you and your plans. The closer we come to the other person's special interests, the closer we rivet their attention.

Look for clues that reveal traits of character and ability. Try to understand what trait lies behind actions that are unusual, even if they seem trivial. And most importantly, use every bit of information about people to prove your genuine interest.

See Them At Their Best

Yesterday morning, I attended a seminar conducted by

a great, long-term friend of mine, Rick. We've been good friends (Master Mind partners) for about ten years. I've sat with him, shared highlights of my life and he's shared highlights of his. We've set goals, celebrated successes, literally hundreds of times. I thought I knew him. Well, I did know him, but, yesterday, as I watched him make a brilliant presentation, I realized that I really didn't know him. Or, putting it another way, I had described him to myself prior to yesterday morning in a way which was inadequate. I was limiting him. There was more about Rick than I knew and as a result I couldn't describe him fully. And, even now, if I'm ever to describe Rick, I still could not describe him as fully in terms of his capabilities and strengths as he deserves. The lesson I learned from this experience is that we never really know each other. There is more excellence, potential and quality inside each of us than we ever really know.

Get to know—really know—those in your life. Find time to see them at their best. And, when you see them at their best—*really* look at them to become aware of how remarkable they are. The benefit you will gain is a greater awareness of your team, your team's assets. You'll play off your team's strengths. And by playing off your team's strengths, you will create synergistic power.

Advancement

Jan told our Leadership Development Lab, "I've had a problem with Irene for the last three years. She really resented my being promoted to supervisor of the accounting department. She had been employed with the firm for several years before I joined the company and she expected the promotion herself.

"I have talked with her several times in the last few weeks to see what her main concerns are. I have listened to what she says and doesn't say. I've shown her that I care about her concerns and how she feels. I've stopped by her desk every day to see how she is doing and ask about things that concern her area of responsibility. I've made a point of writing her notes about the things she does well or even about her looking especially nice that day. I really tried to put myself in her shoes. I treated her like I want to be treated.

"I can see a definite improvement not only in her work but also, more importantly, in her attitude. She still doesn't really like me being her supervisor, but she feels a lot better about herself and about me. She even said 'thank you' in a note she left on my desk."

What can we learn from this simple story? People have feelings. Whether we agree with their feelings or not, they own those feelings—those attitudes. We can sit in judgment and say, "She's a jerk," or accept responsibility as an empowering leader to help change her attitude. You *can* help change attitudes. Don't cop out. Reread the above example. Look at the situation. It could have been a real stalemate and considered hopeless—impossible. But it wasn't hopeless, it wasn't impossible. Jan accepted her responsibility as a leader to influence performance by first of all taking the responsibility to understand her new subordinate and secondly stepping back from her own ego—her own need to be "the boss" and in control. Jan "let the other person feel important."

How about you? Is there a tough person in your life who needs your help in changing her attitude—someone whose cooperation you need—someone whose respect you need? Here is the paradox: To gain that person's cooperation and respect, you begin by cooperating with her desire to feel important—you begin to earn her respect by expressing a genuine interest in her.

In relating to and leading others ask yourself these major questions:

Do they have the habit of compensating for a sense of inferiority—

- By rising to a dare?
- By strutting? Are they a peacock, vain about almost everything?
- By boasting?
- By putting up a false front of confidence?
- By being arrogant, superior and quarrelsome?
- By responding unfavorably to suggestions? Are they "negative?"
- Or are they really big people who welcome suggestions and criticisms?
- Do they have a "pet vanity?" If so, what is it?
- If they have a swelled head, are they covering up a sense of inferiority? Or do they represent the rare type, the grown-up spoiled child, with a genuine superiority feeling who must at times be handled roughly and whom it is dangerous to praise?
- Do they shirk responsibility or do they seek it?
- Are they clever or dull?

The objectives and goals of your organization, your team, must come first, and everyone, including those reporting to you, must recognize this. It is in helping, caring for and about others, that we best reach our organization's objectives and goals. Do everything you can to help your team members and make their work life easier. You will empower your team and every member on it. You will know the joy of true leadership.

You like to be in on things. You like your supervisors to take you into their confidence and keep you informed. When they don't, it doesn't make you feel very important, or very enthusiastic about cooperating, does it? So why in the world should the people who work for you and for me feel any different?

Empowering leaders try to keep their people fully informed at all times. It's an important part of their jobs, so they take it seriously and try to do it well. They know that when information stops, rumors start. They want cooperation, not just compliance; keeping people well informed, promptly, is an essential way to express genuine interest..

If you want results in dealing with people you must become genuinely interested in them.

o   o   o

Become Genuinely Interested

I watched them tear a building down.
A gang of men in a busy town.
With ho-heave-ho and a lusty yell,
They swung a beam and the side wall fell.
I asked the foreman, "Are these men skilled
As the men you'd hire if you had to build?"

He gave a laugh and said, "No, indeed,
Just common labor is all I need.
I can easily wreck in a day or two,
What builders have taken a year to do."
And I thought to myself as I went my way,
Which of these roles have I tried to play?

Am I builder who works with care,
Measuring life by the rule and square?
Am I shaping my deeds to a well-made plan?
Patiently doing the best I can?
Or am I a wrecker, who walks the town
Content with the labor of tearing down.

Author Unknown

$$>>> 8$$

Avoid Criticism

*"Don't judge any man
until you have walked two moons
in his moccasins."*

American Indian Proverb

Think Twice Before Attacking

Last night, at about ten o'clock, armed with flashlights, pick and shovel, Loren (our youngest son) and I set out to solve the persisting problem that's been bothering us all summer— yellow jackets landing on our plates when we ate outside on the deck. We began to dig in the area of our deck where the yellow jackets have been coming from. We dug down about three feet when we heard this, "buzz-buzz-buzz." Yikes! Then I felt a bee on my forehead. I yelled. Loren yelled. We began to run as fast as we could for the back door of the house. Several stings later, we were secure in our house.

What the yellow jackets did was perfectly natural. They attacked back. They tried and successfully protected their home, their turf, their territory. You and I are a lot like yellow jackets.

If we feel attacked, we'll defend ourselves, fight back, and somebody's going to get hurt. In the act of trying to defend ourselves, someone always gets hurt. And anytime anyone feels attacked, the most natural thing is to fight back. Think twice before you attack anyone, criticize anyone, even if you think they may not respond. The benefit you'll gain is: Cemented, strengthened relationships with your empowered team.

Criticism is the easiest way to handle an irritation or discouragement. There seems to be a continuous controversy over how to use criticism, if indeed we should use it at all. Benjamin Franklin said, "I will speak ill of no man and speak all the good I know of everybody." Our natural tendency is to criticize, condemn and complain. The problem with criticism is that it seldom works, it almost always invokes a defensive reaction. Criticism never results in teamwork and doesn't bring out the best in people. Criticism causes others to justify their actions. So, one of the first recommendations for being an empowering leader is to develop your ability to withhold judgement and criticism.

Some people feel that criticism is a resource—a leadership tool. Criticism is an unconscious habit, and we may think that some people need it. We may think there is no other way. But criticism builds resentment. Subconsciously, many of us think people will take advantage of us if we do not criticize. The truth is, criticism is dangerous. Criticism is demeaning and it hurts a person's sense of pride. We never notice how much criticism hurts unless we're on the receiving end. Criticism invariably makes people strive to justify themselves. You may think, "Yes, but I want to reach people! They don't listen unless you criticize." Criticism is like homing pigeons and boomerangs: it always comes back and sometimes catches you on the backside. Avoid using it. "He who criticizes gets little cooperation." Who chooses to follow a leader who is negative and critical?

Criticism cuts off communication, productivity, creativity and job satisfaction. Criticism causes the receiver to "feel" and not listen. Criticism can easily sabotage a positive working environment. Criticism is a way of discussing what is not working that fixes blame on the person who did something "wrong." Criticism questions the competence or character of the person, instead of focusing attention on an activity or performance. The result is demoralizing and disempowering: people feel less able to get the job done. Criticism suppresses enthusiasm and a willingness to participate.

Have You Noticed?

Mike was working hard at trying to get two of his team members to work more cooperatively together. They did not seem to talk civilly, respect each other, or show any signs of cooperating with each other. Mike was heading down the stairs of his office building, from one floor to the next (a high-tech manufacturing company), when he heard at the bottom of the stairway, around the corner, a couple of voices. To his surprise and pleasure, it was his two team members.

When he heard the voices, he slowed his pace. He was so curious to hear what they were talking about he stopped before they could sense his presence to eavesdrop on them for a moment. What he heard was not what he wanted to hear. It was probably not what you would want to hear either. But it was probably the most important lesson in leadership that Mike has ever received. This is what he heard:

"Mike is our biggest problem around here."

"You're not kidding. All he ever does when he comes into my area is criticize. First thing he says is, 'Have you noticed...?' and right after that is something he wants me to change, some piddly, trifling, insignificant thing he wants changed. He never says that he's noticed improvements or gains, or that he's noticed where we've made progress."

The other person responded, "It's become a joke in our department. Everybody looks at each other when he says, 'Have you noticed…?' because they realize some form of criticism is going to follow."

Mike quietly walked back up the stairs with something to think about. That night, when he got home, he asked his wife, "Do I ever notice things around here?" And she said, "Do you ever notice things around here?! That's all you ever do is notice things around here."

Fortunately for Mike, those two coworkers helped him see his tendency to criticize and complain. It had become such an ingrained habit—such an unconscious behavior—that Mike was totally unaware of it. This inclination to complain and criticize can easily become a habit for any of us.

Critic's Vacation

I met with a new class member. He was scheduled to start our Leadership Lab the following Thursday. We visited for a few minutes, and I said, "You've got a pretty active 'critic.' You'll need to leave your critic out of the class room if you're going to gain full value from the experience—if you're going to gain full value from the Leadership Lab." His response was, "You're very insightful. I do have an active critic." Well, most of us do.

If you want to experience a lift, let your critic take a vacation or maybe a leave of absence. Give your critic—that part of your personality, that tendency to analyze, scrutinize, criticize, critique, that cynical analyzer—give that part of your personality a couple of weeks off. You may be amazed at how much fun you'll have. And, you know what? Giving your critic a few weeks off will help you break through to new heights as a leader.

"It Is Not The Critic"

It is not the critic who counts
Nor the man who points out how the
strong man stumbled
Or where the doer of deeds could have
done better
The credit belongs to the man who is
actually in the arena
Whose face is marred by dirt, sweat
and blood
Who strives valiantly, who errs and
comes short again and again
Who knows a great enthusiasm, a
great devotion
And spends himself in a worthy cause
Who at the best knows in the end the
triumph of high achievement
And who at the worst if he fails at least
fails while daring greatly
So that his place shall never be with
those cold and timid souls
Who know neither victory nor defeat.

Criticizing Diminishes Teams

John told our Leadership Development Lab, about his experience with his son's little-league team, a few years ago. The head coach was a perfectionist—demanding that all of the boys play like men. He criticized any mistake, lost his temper regularly, and, finally, after a losing game, told the boys that they were "losers" and he quit. This left John and another inexperienced father to coach the team for the remainder of the season. The team was in last place. The new coaches began to encourage the team. By the end of the season, they were number six in the league, they made the playoffs, and it didn't stop there. They won the first playoff game, the second, then beat all the teams who'd beaten them earlier in the season. You guessed it—they took first place in their league.

The lesson we can learn from this experience is that criticizing/complaining diminishes people and teams—actually holds people back, disempowers, robs people of their strengths. Praise and encourage every member of your team. Be hearty in your approbation. Be lavish in your praise.

Condemning

Talking behind the back of others borders on immorality and is always demoralizing to the speaker and the listener. Other people may be totally wrong, but they don't think so!! Do not condemn them; any fool can condemn. Instead, try to understand them. If you find the reason why they think and act the way they do, you'll have the key to their actions. Ask yourself, "How would I feel, how would I react if I were in their shoes?"

Sunday, after church, our son took us out for Mothers' Day lunch. The line was backed up. We waited and waited and waited. The manager looked at us and said, in sort of a critical, demeaning way, pointing at the girl who was supposed to take our order, "She's new."

She's new, so what? Who trained her? Who selected her? Am I, the customer, supposed to suffer, train her, or is that the job of her manager, who was belittling and condemning her, projecting, trying to focus away from himself and his responsibility?

The lesson I learned from this experience is the importance of never condemning another member of my team to the outside world. We talk to each other openly. We resolve our differences behind closed doors. To the outside world, we speak with one voice. Resolve, today, to be open with your team, to allow for feedback and coaching and to never speak unfairly of a fellow team member to the outside world—to the outside customer—behind his back. The benefit you'll gain is an empowered team, and this empowered team will help you be further empowered.

Don't be one of the people described below:

Lord Chesterfield said, "Nine in ten of every company you are with will avail themselves of every indiscreet and unguarded expression of yours if they can turn it to their own advantage."

Oprah Winfrey said, "If your people stab you in the back—rid yourself of them."

Empowering leaders have learned how to forgive and forget. Empowering leaders do not hold grudges or resentments. As a result they gain personal empowerment which in turn empowers the team. Giving up authority and developing the willingness to watch other people fail and start over again does require patience. It is a virtue worth cultivating.

Inspector

Jeff, who is president of a custom alloy metal fabricating company, told our Leadership Development Lab about John, an inspector for one of his customers, who had been in the custom alloy metal fabricating business for himself before his business failed. John liked to tell everyone how to do their job, making him come across like a know-it-all.

"Once when we were working on a large six-month project," Jeff said, "several of us struggled with the feeling that we could never quite measure up to John's expectations. This made the job we were working on become a real pain. During this time I became friends with one of John's co-workers, and we began joking about John's manner of 'helping.' We both agreed that he was a real 'ass' to work with or even to be around.

"About two months after we completed the job, I was on another construction site watching the installation of one of our tanks. While I was in the portable construction office I overheard some of the engineers from John's company talking, and someone mentioned that one of the other inspectors was acting a lot like John. Without thinking I said in a joking manner, 'What, you mean acting like an ass?' The whole office went quiet. I knew I had struck a nerve. I knew that I had put my foot in my mouth. I did my best to make a joke out of it, then I went on about my business. I felt awkward, to say the least.

"Nothing ever came of my remark until about six weeks later when I received a call from John who said, 'Hello, this is your favorite ass.' Unfortunately because of my mistake there are real problems in our relationship, and I am still struggling to get John's approval on some of our work.

"The lesson I learned was to never, ever put someone down in public—even if you are trying to make a joke out of it. Because it will backfire on you."

Complaining

Tom told our Leadership Development Lab a great story about complaining. "After learning and memorizing the Leadership Principles and making them a permanent part of my brain, I took them home. My first challenge occurred soon after I walked in the back door of my home. I must relearn thinking and speaking if I am going to communicate with my wife without violating principle number three—Don't Criticize, Condemn or Complain. No more criticism. This required impromptu, innovative thinking to organize my thoughts in a totally positive manner. I have been guilty of what I used to call "positive criticism." I have knowingly used it on my wife for years in regard to keeping the catsup bottle out of the refrigerator. I like catsup warm. All my comments to her about the catsup have gone unheeded because the catsup is still kept in the refrigerator. The lesson I learned is that criticism in any form is not effective. The action I want you to take is to express your thoughts to others in positive terms, and your benefit will be a positive response."

Complaining takes the sweetness out of life and relationships. Who wants to be around, much less follow, the dull-minded, negative person who sees and points out the little imperfections that always exist?

Too hot, too cold, too fast, too slow, too big, too little, too short, too tall, too dry, too wet, too skinny, too fat—One of the ways you can set yourself apart, distinguish yourself from others, is by refraining from the common behavior of complaining with uncomplimentary adjectives.

Publicity

Yesterday morning, I watched a friend of mine who is a public figure stand in front of several thousand people and joke about a critical newspaper article aimed at her. "It would have cost me $30,000 to get this publicity." she said. The article was filled with half-truths and, from my perspective, misrepresents certain very important points. Yet, when she spoke about it she remained centered, dignified and graceful.

Winston Churchill said, "So long as I'm acting from duty and conviction, I'm indifferent to taunts and jeers. I think they will probably do me more good than harm."

Today, you may be on the receiving end of criticism. The more we do, the more we innovate, the more we attempt to improve things, the more efforts we make toward improvements of any kind, the more likely, the more certain, ridicule and judgement become. So when criticism comes, be grateful for it. When you stop worrying about criticism, you exercise a new kind of freedom and personal power that can never be known when your every act is measured to win the approval of others.

So, today, act bravely and welcome criticism.

Elbert Hubbard has some good advice:

"It is foolish to say sharp, hasty things, but it is a deal more foolish to write 'm. When a man sends you an impudent letter, sit right down and give it back to him with interest ten time compounded—and then throw both letters in the wastbasket."

There Must Be A Better Way

Criticizing, condemning, and complaining are to be replaced by coaching, correcting and when necessary reprimanding. The focus is on bringing forth each person's excellence so that the job gets done—not judging the individual as incompetent or bad when their performance is less than satisfactory. When done properly, the discussion of what is not working moves the work forward and encourages participation.

> *"People may ask you for criticism,*
> *But they really want praise."*
> William Somerset Maugham

*"Any fool can criticize, condemn and complain—
and most fools do."*
Benjamin Franklin

"Do not judge and you will never be mistaken."
Rousseau

o   o   o

**Never Be Quick To Judge,
Withhold Criticism!
Never Speak Critically Of Another Person Behind Their
Back,
Don't Condemn!
Give Your Attention To The Little Things You Like,
Don't Be A Complainer!**

If I Were Boss

If I were boss I would like to say;
"You did a good job here today."
I'd look for a man, or a girl or boy
Whose heart would leap with a thrill of joy
At a word of praise, and I'd pass it out
Where the crowd could hear as I walked about.

If I were boss I would like to find
The fellow whose work is the proper kind;
And whenever to me a good thing came
I'd like to be told the toiler's name,
And I'd go to him, and I'd pat his back,
And I'd say, "That was perfectly splendid, Jack!"

Now a bit of praise isn't much to give
But it's dear to the hearts of all that live;
And there's never a man on this good old earth
But is glad to be told when he's been of worth;
And a kindly word, when the work is fair,
Is welcome and wanted everywhere.

If I were boss I'm sure I would
Say a kindly word whenever I could
For a man who has given his best by day
Wants a little more than his weekly pay;
He likes to know with the setting sun,
That his boss is pleased with the work he's done.

Author Unknown

>>>9

Acknowledgement

"The deepest principle of human nature
Is the craving to be appreciated."
William James

Acknowledgement of individuals' contributions to the organization is a process that will increase the effectiveness of the total effort immeasurably. In the past organizations treated people as if they were wage slaves. Workers who punched a clock and were paid based on the hours they contributed to the job were regarded as units of production. The personality of the individual, his desires, interests, dreams and hopes were of no importance to the organization. The worker was supposed to check invoices, or operate a screw machine, or place rivets in an assembly almost automatically. Those who sought acknowledgment were considered to be troublemakers. Those who expected a pat on the back or credit for a job well done often were discarded for workers who performed their jobs by rote and never complained or demanded recognition.

Empowering leaders recognize in every situation, regardless of their position, that part of their job is to create an atmosphere that builds people. We create an atmosphere that builds people, that brings out the best in people, by practicing the four steps to effective acknowledgement. Most of us are not in the habit of giving acknowledgement. We all tend to take others for granted. You bring out the best in the others by helping them see themselves as more capable and empowering them to aim higher, achieve greater things, and believe even more in themselves. The four steps to effective acknowledgement are paying positive attention, giving effective approval, giving effective appreciation, and giving effective praise.

Things have changed, and yet in dozens of companies, management still has failed to learn the lesson of the value of individual recognition.

Groceries

Not too long ago I had a cup of coffee with a 52-year-old district manager who has been responsible for a large number of stores in a half state area for a major food retail chain. George has been with the company for many years. He took over his current area when it was losing $500,000 dollars per year. For the last several years the territory has averaged a profit of two million dollars.

George was recently told that he would have to be happy with his job responsibilities as they currently exist. In other words, he has been shelved for the balance of his career. George seems to have resolved himself to the company decision and has worked out for himself things he can do for his own growth and development. This will ensure a freshness about his life, whether or not any advancement in his career comes. He also knows what he can expect in income, based on this kind of career path over the balance of the 13 years he will work. He's an energetic man, he loves to work and doesn't look forward to retirement.

George's complaint about the company, surprisingly, wasn't that he's been shelved; his complaint was that he gets no recognition for the job he did of taking his area from a losing position to the profits it now enjoys. He feels that the only interaction he has with management focuses on what he's doing wrong, what isn't right, what needs to be done, what can be done, and so on. Yet there's no recognition for the outstanding job he has done. It's not an unusual story.

Unfortunately, it's a very common condition and it is the most common complaint I encounter when I visit with managers of client companies. What may be a little surprising to me, is that this lack of recognition, is not limited to any give level of a company. Instead, I find that regardless of the level of the folks within an organization, the need for and the lack of recognition seems to be all up and down the ladder.

Note

I visited with the vice president of a client company three weeks ago. He reached over on his desk, to a note that he had received from the president of the company, a note of encouragement, recognition, praise, and appreciation; and with some pride showed it to me. These two men had worked together for almost 30 years. They obviously know each other very well, but the pride that the executive vice president took in the note he received from the president of the company was genuine and the importance of the note was significant.

Aren't we all sensitive to the acknowledgment of others? Isn't it a fact that we expand ourselves and our efficiency when we're complimented, told that we are important, valuable and essential to the success of our company?

Pay Positive Attention

If people reject your "approval," then you have not earned the right. Start by paying attention to them. Giving approval to someone to whom attention has not been paid is like running directly to second base and skipping first base entirely. People reject our approval or appreciation when we have not earned the right by first paying positive attention. Effective attention is accomplished through warmly acknowledging others and observing and listening to them without judging. For instance, we say "Good morning, how are you doing?" Pay attention to people for "showing up." They earn positive attention for being present.

On his way home from the theater one cold January night, Burch Foraker, head of the Bell Telephone System, descended into a manhole. Was there a crisis? Was he worried over some grave difficulty? Nothing of the sort. He remembered that a couple of his cable splicers were working down in the manhole on a hurry-up job. He just dropped in on them to have a little chat. Foraker became known as the "man of ten thousand friends." He was forever visiting his people at their work in the spirit of camaraderie. It was his way of showing that he considered their jobs important.

Ads

Tanya told our Leadership Development Lab an excellent story about paying effective attention. Friday she had one person price an ad. The next morning she had another person proof the ad confirming that everything was priced correctly. The night person tagged the ad and proofed it against the items on the shelf. The opening clerk would put out the ad flyers and post the ad on the day the ad ran. Tanya checked up on them by phone or by coming in to the store. Tanya did this a few times, showing that she really cared. It also encouraged the employees to do it right because there would be a follow-up.

Tanya said the lesson she learned is the importance of continual praise and follow up with her team. They like to know what they are doing wrong and what they are doing right everyday so they know where they stand. Tell your employees every day how well they are doing and how important they are to you. You will all understand each other, work together and experience the empowerment of synergistically working toward one goal.

Pay Day

Kevin told our class a fabulous story about the power of paying positive attention. He said he was challenged by the difficulty of getting commitments from electricians he hires from the Union Hall. To solve his problem, Kevin began to utilize the principle of paying positive attention—greeting the electricians in the morning, learning their names and then calling them by name. When it came time to give them their paychecks, instead of the perfunctory process of placing them in the paycheck slot, he made it a point to give them out personally, including a little note—some word of thanks. Kevin said the practice hasn't solved all of his motivation problems, but he's noticed a decided improvement in commitment in some cases, surprising improvements on the part of many.

Management By Wandering Around

There is a "new" school of thought devoted to the concept of MBWA— Management by Wandering (or Walking) Around. In 1985, Tom Peters and Nancy Austin wrote a whole chapter about MBWA in their bestselling book, *In Search Of Excellence*. The point is simple. Get out of your office and pay attention. The higher up you are, the more important it is.

Recently, we conducted the Leadership Lab for 30 supervisors of a 250-person manufacturing plant. The company was facing major morale problems, and the plant was losing money. The first time I visited the corporate office and talked with the human resource director, he happened to mention that the president did not want to visit the company's local plant just across the parking lot because he was afraid it might show preferential treatment, he also avoided the plants in Louisiana, Toronto and Vancouver, B.C., because they might think he was showing favoritism.

Six months after the completion of the Leadership Lab, the plant supervisor asked me to conduct a follow-up session for the supervisors who were in the original program. The personnel manager said to expect six or eight people. Twenty showed up. He had to drag in a lot of extra chairs. A few people commented to me in tones of shock and surprise that the president of the company had come out of his "ivory tower" and visited the plant floor, shaking hands and talking with the workers. His positive attention had a decidedly positive impact on morale.

I sat across from Bill, yesterday, at lunch. Bill's the president of an astonishing, wholesale tool distributor here in the Portland area. His sales have gone from six to more than 28 million dollars in the last seven years. In response to being asked about his work, his routine, Bill said, "Well, I'm not a real good decision-maker anymore, I don't get a chance to make very many decisions." Then someone asked him what he does with his time, how he spend his time? He said, "I spend a lot of my time wandering around and talking with our people, checking up on *us*, asking for their ideas about how I'm doing and how the company's doing and what we can do to make their job easier."

He said, "I may not be making a lot of decisions any-more, but I'm a lot smarter since I started managing by wander-ing around.

"Well, Bill, you may not be making a lot of decisions anymore, but you've made the most important decision any leader can make, and that decision is to empower your people and push decisions to the lowest possible level.

How about you? Do you need to have your finger in every pie, micromanage every area? Today would be a great day to release a little. Ask others how *you're* doing instead of *telling them* how they're doing.

You may be astounded at what you learn.

One of the most dangerous practices with anyone on your team is to ignore them. We all do a better job when we feel someone is paying attention and cares about our work.

Home Coming

Praise at any level of human interaction works the same. Yesterday afternoon, at our Turbo Sales Lab, Jim told us that he'd been making a point of greeting his kids when he got home from work with a smile and a compliment before he jumped on them about incomplete chores. He said that he'd fallen into the habit of starting in on them the minute he walked in the house. I asked him what difference his new attitude had made—what difference he had noticed? He said his kids seemed to like him better. He said, "My wife noticed the difference right away." He said, "I even like myself better."

The lesson I've learned from Jim's report is how easy it is to fall into the habit of complaining and griping about things and how this spoils and takes any joy out of our relationships. The action I call you to is: Begin with praise. Look for and find ways to praise those you love. The benefit you'll gain is enduring relationships.

Make My Day

Sunday, as we were leaving church, we followed a four-year-old girl. She was holding the hand of her daddy. I said to her, "Those are beautiful purple shoes." She didn't turn around, she kept walking, but she kind of looked up at her dad and he looked down at her and smiled. My wife said, "That's a beautiful heart on the back of your jacket." And again, she sort of looked up at her dad. I never did see her face; her dad turned around and said, "You've made her whole day." We didn't break our stride; I only expressed what I was thinking and feeling and she had glowed, reflecting her pride to her dad.

Wow, not much of an investment to make someone's whole day. All I had to do was express my feelings. All I had to do was express my sense of appreciation, my sense of value, an expression of approval.

Think about the power, think about the opportunity that you have today. You can make someone's whole day. All it takes is a pleasant word. People may not show it as readily as a four-year-old little girl, but, inside each of us, there's a four-year-old who's waiting to hear a word of approval, a word of appreciation, a word of caring. So, if you'd like to experience the power of making a difference, why not look for someone "in pretty little purple shoes?" Or, better yet, look for someone who's trying hard to do his job well, and tell them you admire their effort.

Wake Up The Giant

I had a hard time sleeping last night. When I got home, at about 10 p.m. from doing a talk for CSI, I found a message from Nada. It was a little late, but I felt like I should return her call. When she answered, she said, "Larry, I finished your book, *Repeat Business,* on my flight to San Francisco. I loved it. I want 50 copies for my people." I said, "Wow, thank you. Your support means so much to me." She said, "No, there's more. I showed it to my boss, my manager. He liked it too. I think he wants to buy 250 copies for all of our West Coast reps." I said, "Wow, thank you. Thank you." She said, "No, wait, there's more. My manager asked me if you could speak for our annual customer service conference? You know, we're having our meeting in Portland this year—our annual West Coast meeting. Maybe you could come and be our speaker,'" she said.

I said "Nada, this means so much to me." I was so stimulated, I could hardly go to sleep.

Well, the lesson I learned is the power of positive feedback, especially in those areas where we're unsure of ourselves—where we've made a major effort, a major commitment. Nada made my day, made my week, made my month.

Look for someone who's putting themselves into a new effort—into some thing they are unsure of, some place they have made a real commitment. And, if you like what they have done, **tell them so.** Tell them so with feeling. You'll make their whole day. They may not be able to sleep, but you'll sleep like a baby.

"Pay attention for showing up."

Give Effective Approval

Approval is acknowledging people with acceptance and encouragement. For example: "You did good," "Keep it up," "That's the way," etc. Say it in three words or less.

Effective approval is when the receiver accepts the approval from the giver. The giver must watch, observe, and ask to make sure the receiver accepts the approval. Otherwise, the giver doesn't know if the approval was effective. To be effective in our leadership role we must become aware of even the slightest improvements in performance. Notice them, acknowledge them, praise them.

Bob had a "social butterfly" on his crew who was not getting his job done. Bob decided to get to know the operator better. He started his deliberate campaign of paying attention and giving approval at every opportunity—whenever the operator was doing something even approximately right. A few days later, Bob had his weekend off. On the morning of his second day off, his phone rang. It was his replacement supervisor, Bruce, who said, "What have you done? I can't believe the change in our social butterfly!" The "social butterfly" had worked thirteen sets instead of his usual eight—a sixty-two percent increase—setting a new "personal best" for himself. The operator has since exceeded his "personal best" three times. Too often we feel we should not give approval for doing things "approximately right." We think people have already been paid for doing the job.

Empowering leaders have learned to always praise every improvement—even the slightest improvement. We tend to look for perfection. We focus in on the blemish—the little flaw. We feel that by drawing attention to the imperfect, we will get improved performance—better work. Yet, the opposite is true. We breed resentment and dissatisfaction—our team is demoralized and disempowered. So, instead of drawing attention to every little mistake, draw attention to every improvement, the slightest improvement. Do not expect your subordinates to be perfect in everything. They will not be. Use their strengths to help them to overcome their weaknesses.

The great majority of people we deal with have an inferiority feeling. To some extent they are uneasy about themselves or their work. Effective encouragement helps build self-confidence, courage and, in the process, improves performance. A pat on the back, though only a few vertebrae removed from a kick in the pants, is miles ahead in results.

Give approval for being approximately right!

Give Effective Appreciation!

Appreciation is expressed when a person does something extra. Appreciation is a "thank you for your extra effort—doing more than you are expected to do." Effective appreciation is when the giver observes that the appreciation was accepted by the receiver.

Webster defines "appreciate" as *"to recognize gratefully..."*

For example: "I appreciate your hard work," or "Thank you for putting yourself out." Remember, if they do not accept your appreciation, go back to giving them *just* approval. One of the most pressing problems businesses face today is turnover. I always remind my clients, "People don't turn over. They go down the street and interview a new boss."

Two years ago, Greg, who owns several McDonald's restaurants, made a decision to do something about the unsatisfactory turnover rate his stores were experiencing. Part of his program involved intensive leadership skills training for his supervisors, including helping them learn the importance of giving lots of appreciation. Greg began to chart his stores' turnover rate after the leadership skills training. His twelve-month chart sloped down at a forty-five degree angle. At the end of the 12 months of training he hired as many people in one month as he had been hiring in one day. People stay where they are appreciated.

By complimenting people from time to time in a way which pleases them, you gain their good will. Give them credit for what they do. Show that you consider them important. Let your outstanding trait be "your unfailing recognition and appreciation of ability in any form." Appreciation is a powerful method for stimulating interest and loyalty. To inspire enthusiasm and loyalty in subordinates, share the limelight for successes. Be ready to help shoulder the blame for their mistakes.

"Give appreciation for going the extra mile."

Give Effective Praise

Praise is the oxygen of the soul. When you give praise, you nourish the essence of a person. When you praise you are really giving a raise, a lift to the spirit. Remember how fragile the human ego is. Remember how unsure you have been at times in the past. Remember how scared those within your influence may be.

Praise means telling a person about something you observed her doing or saying that reveals one of her personal traits, a quality in her that is admirable or outstanding. The highest form of praise gives the receiver a thought that builds her self-image. The giver's words stay in the mind of the receiver, affecting her self-esteem. The highest form of praise gives the receiver a positive reputation to live up to. She sees herself in a new light and begins to behave in harmony with this strengthened image.

If with praise we can raise people, and if when things are appreciated they increase in value, it could be said that an organization that expresses appreciation is one which is rich in human resources.

"Focus praise on a quality."

Observe The Good In Others

In one session of the Leadership Development Lab we teach a unit on active listening. It's a fantastic session. After each Lab member makes a short presentation, other class members respond to them—give them a compliment—on one of the strengths they've observed in them based on their presentation. As one of our class members was trying to give this compliment, she said, "I have to think so hard." Yes, we do have to think hard if we're going to be able to come alive, give praise, compliment, produce positive feedback to the important people in our world. There's no lack of excellence in the performance of our customers, suppliers, coworkers, bosses, subordinates, friends and family. The lack of excellence is in our own thinking, our own lack of "thinking hard."

The lesson I've learned is that if I'm going to bring out the best in others, I must be willing to think hard. If I'm going to help others grow and build bonding relationships, I must be willing to think hard, wake up the gray matter, give praise. Wake up your own gray matter, come alive, stir up your thinking, observe the good in others, and give them the positive praise they deserve. The benefits you'll gain are bonding relationships with growing people. You'll build an empowered team. Remember, the most powerful and effective praise points out characteristics or qualities about which the receiver is uncertain.

Jodie was interviewing some of her employees for a position opening up in the paper mill. She utilized the fifteen Leadership Principles during the interviews as a basis for selection. When the interviews were over, she told each interviewee which leadership skills she had observed in them during the interview. This helped make them feel good about them-

selves—whether or not they got the job. Jodie said by telling
them, at the conclusion of their interview, some of their
strengths, they were encouraged about themselves, their potential, and their future with the paper mill.

The one important precaution is this: Remember that
some people, a *minority*, "puff up" under praise and "go to
pieces." Be aware of them. The person who is "puffed up," who
is arrogant and conceited or disagreeable is, in most cases, compensating for a lack of self-esteem or self-confidence. What
people like this really need is praise and encouragement, not
harsh treatment. Safeguard the self-esteem of all people with
whom you want to maintain friendly relations. Protect them
from your own desire to feel superior and important. Remember
that this desire is always at work inside you, whether you realize it or not.

Following are praise-worthy traits and qualities to look
for in people. Most of us can spontaneously list far more negative qualities or traits than we can list positive qualities. The
positive qualities listed below are for your convenience. People
like to be praised. Pick the descriptive words you want to apply
to the team members in your life. You can add to the list as you
think of additional positive qualities.

Remember the most powerful and effective praise
points out qualities and characteristics about which the receiver
is uncertain.

"And to give thanks is good"
Swinburne

Persuasive	Enthusiastic	Soothing	Tolerant
Spontaneous	Friendly	Unselfish	Unruffled
Brave	Adaptable	Impressive	Sociable
Willing	Exciting	Devout	Contented

Proud	Convincing	Direct	Dynamic
Congenial	Discreet	Cheerful	Sensitive
Superior	Expressive	Entertaining	Admirable
Confident	Open-minded	Tenacious	Quick-witted
Inspiring	Venturesome	Outgoing	Agreeable
Generous	Calm	Interesting	Firm
Easy-going	Motivating	Good Mixers	Bright
Talented	Kind	Delightful	Poised
Effective	Ambitious	Soft-hearted	Precise
High-spirited	Unassuming	Gifted	Vigorous
Energetic	Good-natured	Encouraging	Fluent
Happy	Humble	Colorful	Competent
Composed	Enjoyable	Masterful	Cautious
Big-hearted	Receptive	Reflective	Obedient
Refined	Fearless	Excellent	Pleasant
Thoughtful	Careful	Faithful	Empathic
Considerate	Courageous	Eager	Resourceful
Insightful	Aware	Determined	Creative
Insightful	Stimulating	Productive	Decisive
Quick-thinkers		Accommodating	
Communicative			

H. Hobart Porter, the noted public utility man, laid down this rule to guide his treatment of workers: "Give them full and public credit for all they do—praise them in public."

Beethoven's Kiss

The pianist Andor Foldes tells the story of Beethoven's kiss which shows how encouragement and acknowledgement enhance personal performance.

As I was giving a master class for young pianists in Saarbruecken, West Germany, in September 1985, I felt that one student would do even better if given a pat on the back. I praised him before the whole class for what distinguished his playing. He immediately outdid himself, to his amazement and that of the group. A few words brought out the best in him.

How happy and proud the first praise I remember receiving made me feel! I was seven, and my father asked for help in the garden. I worked as hard as I could and was richly rewarded when he kissed me and said, "Thanks, son, you did very well." His words still ring in my ears more than six decades later.

At 16, I was in the midst of a personal crisis arising from differences with my music teacher. Then the renowned pianist, Emil von Sauer, Liszt's last surviving pupil, came to Budapest and asked me to play for him. He listened intently to Bach's Toccata in C major and requested more. I put all my heart into playing Beethoven's "Pathetique" sonata and continued with Schumann's "Papillons." Finally, von Sauer rose and kissed me on the forehead. "My son," he said, "when I was your age I became a student of Liszt. He kissed me on the forehead after my first lesson, saying, 'Take good care of this kiss—it comes from Beethoven, who gave it to me after hearing me play.' I have waited for years to pass on this sacred heritage, but now I feel you deserve it."

Nothing in my life has meant as much to me as von Sauer's praise. Beethoven's kiss miraculously lifted me out of my crisis and helped me become the pianist I am today. Soon I in turn will pass it on to the one who most deserves it.

Praise is a potent force, a candle in a dark room. It is magic, and I marvel that it always works.

o   o   o

Think of someone with whom you would like to strengthen your relationship, eliminate friction, improve response, or just help grow. What is one of his positive traits or qualities? How could you express to him your admiration or respect of this trait? What could you say? Remember the importance of being specific. Remember that, even though people love to be told that we appreciate them, that we value them, most people are skeptical. Praise that is not accepted is of no real value at all. How will you express praise so that it will be accepted?

Jot down the name of a person with whom you would like to strengthen your relationship, bring out the best, and lead more effectively.

Name of person with whom you would like to strengthen your relationship: _____

What do you like about this person—what are some of his strengths, strong points, good qualities? _____
_____

When did you tell them last? _____

What would happen if you told them you appreciated this trait or quality?_____

When will you do it? _____

> *"Let me be a little kinder,*
> *Let me be a little blinder*
> *To the faults of those around me,*
> *Let me praise a little more."*
> Edgar A. Guest

o o o

Attention
Approval
Appreciation
Praise

Life's Mirror

There are loyal hearts, there are spirits brave,
There are souls that are pure and true;
Then give to the world the best you have,
And the best will come back to you.

Give love, and love to your life will flow,
A strength in your utmost need;
Have faith, and a score of hearts will show
Their faith in your work and deed.

Give truth, and your gift will be paid in kind,
And honor will honor meet;
And the smile which is sweet will surely find
A smile that is just as sweet.

Give sorrow and pity to those who mourn;
You will gather in flowers again
The scattered seeds from your thought outborne
Though the sowing seemed but vain.

For life is the mirror of king and slave,
'Tis just what we are and do;
Then give to the world the best you have
And the best will come back to you.
Madeline S. Bridges

>>>10

See Their Point Of View!

"The choice of a point of view
Is the initial act of a culture."

Jose Ortega y Gasset

Success in gaining cooperation and leading from strength depends on understanding the other person's point of view. Henry Ford said, "If there is any one secret of success, it lies in the ability to get the other person's point of view and see things from his angle as well as your own."

Traditionally, Labor and Management, Production, Engineering, Credit and Sales departments have had different points of view. New college graduates and tenured employees may hold different points of view. When you deal with people whom you wish to lead, consider all of the points of difference that set them apart from others: the traits of their characters, their capacity, their special problems, needs and interests. Treat each person differently in the light of their own nature and viewpoint.

M.D. To Be

Dr. Siebert, a practical psychologist, told me the story of his niece who graduated with honors from the pre-med program at Lewis and Clark College. She is a brilliant girl she studies hard and has an outstanding G.P.A.. During her senior year, her family wanted to know where she was going to medical school. At the last minute she said, "I'm not going." Instead, she decided to become a lab technician. After going through an intensive program—she did outstanding work there, too—she was hired at a medical lab. The prestige, power and income which we associate with being an M.D. aren't nearly as important to her as the freedom she wants so she can go windsurfing in the Columbia Gorge. At first it was hard for the rest of her family to see her point of view.

The four most important words in the vocabulary of an empowering leader are "What do you think?"

When we seek to motivate and win the cooperation of others we must understand their point of view. If they are not motivated by traditional goals and want flexible hours, like Al's niece who didn't want to go to medical school and become an M.D., understand and work with them. A raise in pay, power, or position would not be as motivating as flex time and challenging, stimulating work. When you can anticipate people's wishes, and meet those wishes before they themselves mention them or perhaps before they even fully realize that those wishes exist, you are able to perform as an empowering leader.

William, who is president of a local real estate company, employs a familiar strategy—a device that Napoleon used to discover a person's point of view. William often opens negotiations by "feeling his way." He starts with a comment which commits him to nothing. Which he can easily pass off later on with a smile. At the same time he conveyed his idea to the other person. Obviously, William has one object in mind: He wants to *uncover the other person's point of view* before he himself makes any real proposals.

Maintaining Maintenance

Don told us, "Prior to becoming service supervisor of the Cable Maintenance Department of a phone company in the Northwest, I was informed of a strong feeling of reservation and resentment that some of the Beaverton crew members had about me being elevated into the position. I felt, after hearing the details of the fears and criticisms, that much of it was based on rumor and hear-say. I realized, however, that if we were going to succeed as a team, it would be my responsibility to take the initiative to earn their respect, trust and confidence. I made an earnest effort to change their ideas about me. I met with each crew member on a one-to-one basis—usually out in the field. My intent was to be as open and honest as possible in answering questions and in discussing goals and work expectations. As a result, I scheduled group meetings and specifically asked for collective ideas and input on what was needed for me to do the best job possible.

"By showing a genuine concern for the crew and their feelings, and respect for their judgement and point of view, they were able to voice what, to them, were important issues on things relating to the job. Because of this sincere and honest attempt to develop trust and respect, I felt I was able to change the crew's attitude towards me. I was told by a leader among the group that the crew's fears concerning me were gone, and that I would be able to count on his support as well as other crew members. The lesson I learned was that by being up-front and honestly dealing with others, there is an opportunity to change in a positive way negative preconceptions and opinions. I fully expect my relationship with the cable maintenance crew to be based on understanding, respect and trust."

The good news, during the months following Don's promotion his team had the lowest repeat repair orders in the history of his company.

Be An Active Listener!

A natural extension of understanding the other person's point of view is to become an active listener.

Leaders let the other person talk. They ask them questions. As a result leaders learn attitudes and ideas that might not be aired. If you, as a leader, disagree, do not interrupt. If you do, the other person will not pay attention because he may still have plenty left to say. One of the hardest things to do is listen, especially when you do not fully agree. Listening will pay off significantly. Remember, most people do not listen, so you will be appreciated in the long run when you do.

"The average person talks too much, especially if he has a good command of the language." said Elbert Gary in discussing the strategy of trading and making a deal. "A wise leader keeps a closed mouth." Great leaders have learned to make a fine art of listening. They know listening is far more than mere silence. They not only feel a genuine interest in what people are saying, but even more, they take the trouble to display their interest.

The Work Of Listening

At the close of a ten-hour seminar, I was beat—I mean I was really tired. I fell asleep at 9:00 p.m. and slept through until the alarm went off, at 6:30 the next morning. The way I conducted this particular seminar is really pretty easy on me. The participants are the center of attention, they do 80 percent plus of the talking—they do most of the work. When I talked with the president of the company, who had been intently engaged and actively involved in the seminar all day, he said, "I wasn't tired. It didn't feel like a ten-hour day to me; it felt more like a three-hour day. I was stimulated, invigorated."

Why was I so tired? I asked my wife who'd helped me do the camera work during the seminar session. She said, "Because you listened to *every word*, and listening is work." Of course, she was right. I did listen to every word, and listening is work. For most of us, listening—*really* listening—takes more effort than rambling along.

The action I'd call you to is: Listen, really listen, to those you love, live and work with. You'll empower them. You'll make their time fly.

Rotary Club

When the program for the Eastside Rotary Club began and before I spoke, there were "guest introductions." Club members introduced guests at their tables. When Bob Munger, our associate, was introduced at his table, the club member who introduced him said, "I've only met this gentleman a few moments ago—I don't know him that well. The one thing I can tell you is: He is a good listener." What a great qualification— to be introduced as a good listener. I'd like to have it said of me—that I'm a "good listener." The most important part of leadership (persuasion, and the secret of building relationships) is being a good listener. Good listeners are sought out by people who are in trouble. Good listeners make our best friends. Good listeners are the best salesmen. Good listeners are the best spouses. Good listeners are the best parents. Good listeners are the best. So, let's turn up our listening, turn down our speaking.

Call Back

Steve, an associate of mine, and I arrived at our 11:30 a.m. appointment in downtown Portland. We had been with a prospective client only last Friday, but we were back again. Why? Not to try and sell him anything, and, certainly, not for just some pleasant visit. We were back to be sure we had really listened last Friday, to be sure we really understood the prospective client's desires and needs. We'd outlined our understanding with a few suggestions and several questions. Again, we listened. As it turns out, we were right on with our understanding. There were a couple of points of clarification. We walked out with more confidence, enthusiasm and conviction.

The lesson I learned is the importance of listening, questioning for clarification and that when I do listen and question for clarification, my confidence and determination are enhanced. Take time to really listen and ask questions for clarity. The benefit you'll gain is greater self-confidence, determination, and this determination will help you persist and win.

Grover Cleveland was a good listener. When he was not sympathetic with his caller's views, he still "listened to the point of painfulness," letting the other person do all the talking.

The easiest way to influence people and to impress them favorably is to let them talk about their interests, opinions and problems. Induce them to talk by asking questions. Be certain that the questions you ask display respect for the other person's knowledge. Make it a definite part of your program to listen attentively when others speak to you. Simple enough, isn't it? Yet how many people have we encountered who are so anxious to tell their story that we cannot get a work in edgewise! When you listen to others in your team and acknowledge the validity of their beliefs, you have taken the first step that will let them follow you whether they agree with you wholeheartedly or not. It's easier for people to follow your way of thinking when you've acknowledged their way of thinking by listening.

Customer Council

The manufacturer of quality household hardware I visited recently has been in business over 40 years, has photos in the lobby of all the employees with the tenure of each employee prominently displayed. It was obvious that this firm had little turnover. As the plant manager and I were first getting acquainted, I complimented him on his lack of turnover. He said, "Oh, there are about 16 people whose pictures we haven't put up yet. We are adding to our team."

I said, "It sounds like business is good."

"Yes, sales are up. We have some new lines that are going very well."

As we toured the plant he proudly pointed out the old and new product lines, all of the production systems and equipment—from casting to packaging—and the final gleaming products.

I said, "Tell me more about your new products." And he obliged saying, "We formed a dealer advisory council this past year. We had our first meeting last summer. The dealers on the council gave us some new product ideas we've implemented and our new products generated a significant increase in sales. Our council of customers can walk into our plant any time they want to and talk to anyone on the floor, from the persons who do the casting, to those who do the painting, polishing and packaging."

Wow, I thought, what a great example of listening to the customer, of being customer-driven and of the benefits that can be gained when people really listen and act on advice given. Sales for this company have gone up because the company listened to its customers. Their labor costs have gone down because they have empowered people on the floor and eliminated unneeded layers of management.

Empowering leaders find ways to ask and listen to their customers, both their internal and external customers and they give their employees the recognition they deserve.

Leaders are people with followers. Though this is a simple definition, it's an extremely practical one. Others will want to follow you when they are convinced that you can get them where they want to go. This was demonstrated in the company who framed its employee's pictures in the lobby

Techniques to Improve Your Listening

Following are some listening techniques:

1. Shut up.
   You can't talk and listen at the same time.
2. Recognize that listening is something you do for personal success.
   You don't listen just to be nice to others. Listening earns power, respect and love, and gets you the information you need to be effective.
3. Want to listen better.
   View listening as a small investment of time and energy that produces an enormous return in understanding.

4. Become less self-centered.

You're about the only one who believes that you and what you have to say are more important than the other person and what he or she has to say. Maybe you're wrong.

5. Prepare to listen.

Think about the speaker and the topic in advance when possible. Set goals for what you hope to learn.

6. Work hard at listening.

Most people speak at an average rate of 120 words per minute. The average listening capacity is about 480 words per minute, or four times faster. This differential causes our minds to wander when another person is speaking. If we can give our speaker a little more con centration—say about 200 wpm of our listening capacity—our minds won't wander. We achieve this by making eye contact, by thinking intently about what is being said, by standing or sitting upright, and by asking questions.

7. Check for nonverbal cues.

Look for what the speaker may be telling you through body language. Listen for tone of voice.

8. Hold your fire.

Don't interrupt. Suspend judgments while the person is talking. Pretend that *everything* she is saying is valid (*it is,* in the sense that she believes it) at least until she stops talking. If you begin to get angry and can't listen you may want to consider stopping the person, talk about your anger, then have her proceed.

9. Don't plan your response while the other person is talking.

    You need only a few seconds to think about your response before giving it. The other person will wait for you. There's nothing wrong with a little silence between that person's words and yours. Trust yourself. You will know what to say.

10. Overcome distractions.

    Ignore noisy surroundings. Fight distractions in the situation or in the speaker.

11. When you need to hear everything a person is saying, say to yourself, "Right now, understanding this person's feelings is the most important thing in my life."

    This is the time to focus all of your 480 wpm listening capacity on the speaker. You'll know you've done your job if you are exhausted afterward.

12. Practice making the decisions you need to make about people and events without coming to final conclusions about them.

    Once you have decided what is true or right you spend your energy defending our conclusion, and you're not likely to listen to disagreement with it. It is better to *act*, when you must, while keeping open the possibility that later you might change your mind.

Francois De La Rochefoucauld said: "One of the reasons that we find so few persons rational and agreeable in conversation is that there is hardly a person who does not think more of what he wants to say than of his answer to what is said."

Eight Strategies To Help People Listen To You

1. Picture your goal in advance.
   Know exactly what response you want from your listener. Before you speak, visualize what you want the listener to look like, feel like, and do as a result of your words. In other words, how do you intend to change the listener?

2. Know your audience, large or small.
   Who are they? What do they already know? How much detail do they need? What have they experienced prior to your message? How do they feel? What do they want to hear? Are they paying attention? Do they care about you and what you have to say?

3. Know how you deliver messages.
   Every human being has a unique way of sending messages. What is your individual style? How do your values, thoughts patterns, vocabulary, tone of voice, speech habits, moods, body language, and overall presence affect the meaning listeners receive?

4. Use positive images to paint pictures.
   Use vivid language, tell complete stories, and paint full pictures that listeners can "see" with their ears. Use examples, metaphors, and analogies. Use fewer word and steer clear of euphemistic language. Choose words that convey specific, concrete images.

5. Show your listeners that you care.
   Show your conviction, confidence and enthusiasm through tone of voice and body language. Don't over-qualify, excessively preface, or apologize for messages as you send them. Shun exaggeration and overstatement. Appeal to the self-interest of your listeners, who continually ask, "What's in it for me?"

6. Make your listeners feel important.

Leave your listeners feeling good about themselves and about you. Be supportive and caring. Don't accuse, belittle, violate expectations, or over-generalize. Be a good listener to your listeners. Use their names in your message. Make them glad they listened to you.

7. Time the readiness of your messages.

Send messages when listeners are ready for them and feel the need for them—not when you want to send them. Choose a location that is consistent with and reinforces the meaning you wish to convey.

8. Critique your results honestly.

What are your listeners telling you? What did they do as a result of your message? Have you been understood? Why or why not? What will you do differently next time?

> *"It is the disease of not listening ...*
> *That I am troubled with."*
> William Shakespeare

Play Yourself Down

An integral part of empowering leadership and improving communication with people in your organization is to play yourself down. There is no limit to what you can achieve if you do not care who gets the credit.

Our challenge as leaders is to display confidence and courage. We also must be realistic models that people will eagerly, enthusiastically and confidently follow. There is a subtle paradox in a style of leadership which admits fallibility. Strong, competent leaders who willingly play themselves down are leaders who others eagerly raise up. When you are acting as a leader in an enterprise or inducing others to carry out your plans, keep yourself in the background whenever possible. Make it clear that you consider the project at hand far more important than yourself. When you deal with team members, be careful to put established cultural practices and policies ahead of your personal views for the moment.

Give your subordinates full credit for the successes of your team. Avoid pretension of any kind and a joke on yourself is often an effective means of gaining attention and goodwill and of disarming any hostility.

In discussing the reason why people fail or succeed, Edward, the president of The National Bank of Minneapolis, said: "One of the things I like to see ... is a person at the head of a business with a lot of strong people around them. If a leader will not select strong assistants, possibly for fear they may displace him or not do as he says, the leader is not a big enough person to be at the head of a big business. Strong leaders will not always do just as they are told, to be sure. But it is not easy to run a business today with a convention of parrots. In a vigorous, growing organization, a great many fairly important decisions are left to people in subordinate positions. You can't have a healthy big business in any other way."

Be ready to sacrifice your vanity when you choose assistants and friends and in your contact with them. Try to find subordinates abler than yourself—even when they realize it. Choose friends whom you can admire and look up to.

Trainee

Debra had a new employee who was making mistakes and wouldn't ask for help. Initially, Debra was focusing on the mistakes. She began to praise the new employee and play herself down when the new secretary made mistakes. The new secretary is now willing to ask questions and ask for help. She is working harder and willing to say she needs help.

To establish a good reputation and gain the respect of others keep in mind that modesty and sound self-promotion go hand in hand. Take special care to be modest about those things you have done, or those qualities you possess which are already recognized, or which are bound to be noticed. Remember that the credit which others give you on their own accord is always greater than any credit which you may gain by claiming it yourself. Try to be modest and establish a reputation for modesty.

Don't efface yourself completely. If some of your worthwhile achievements or traits are fairly certain to be overlooked altogether or not recognized in any way, see to it that they come to the attention of the right people at the right time.

> *"The greater thou art, the more humble thyself."*
> The Apocrypha

Remember, we *lead* when we *deserve* leadership, not because it is given to us.

Abraham Lincoln was once visited by a pessimistic acquaintance who detailed Lincoln's struggles and disappointments in leadership, and then asked, "Honestly, Abe, doesn't this job of being a leader sometimes frighten you?"

"Honestly, why should it?" Lincoln replied. "The trust the people have placed in me doesn't leave any time for fear." Keep your eyes on a *high goal*—merit the trust of those with whom you work—and leadership will become a way of life.

Independent Thinker

A young executive friend of ours is extremely capable, but he is also an independent thinker, and, occasionally, a bit impatient. We asked him recently if this had caused him any problems in his organization, where he seems to be making excellent progress.

"Not really," he said. "Fortunately my boss is very understanding."

Recently the young man went to see his boss to ask to be relieved of membership on a policy committee where his views often disagreed with those of more senior members. "I'm sorry," he told his boss, "but when I disagree with something strongly, it goes against my nature to sit by and say nothing, or act as if I approve. Life might be a lot easier for everyone if I weren't on the committee."

"I'd prefer that you stay on the committee, Bill," said his boss. "You think clearly and express yourself well. I'm always interested in what you think, especially when you disagree with me. When you disagree, you help us see and consider the other side of the picture. That's a big help. Don't underestimate its importance to me and to the company."

The point Bill's boss made to him is probably the best argument for putting yourself in the position of seeing the other person's point of view.

o   o   o

**See The Other Person's Point Of View
Be An Active Listener
Play Yourself Down.**

*The creative is the place where no one
else has ever been,
You have to leave the city of your
comfort and go into the wilderness of
your intuition.
You can't get there by bus, only by
hard work and risk.
And by not quite knowing what you're
doing.
What you'll discover will be wonderful.
What you'll discover will be yourself.*
Alan Alda

>>>11

Leveraging The Ideas Of Others

*"If you go through life
Convinced that your way is always best,
All the new ideas in the world will pass you by."*

Akio Morita, Chairman,
Sony Corporation

I may argue with your ideas and conclusions; I may find fault with your thinking; I may play the devils advocate with your suggestions, but I will defend to the death *my* ideas, *my* conclusions, *my* insights, *my* hunches.

Muddy

A great way to help people to bring out the best in themselves is to encourage them to try their own ideas. Dick Stencil, an earth moving construction crew foreman, told our Leadership Development Lab a story that demonstrates what happens when someone gets a chance to put this idea into action:

"One of my operators had been very reluctant to contribute his ideas to solving the operating problems on the job. He wanted me to come up with all the ideas. When he returned to work after we had been delayed by bad, rainy weather, we were confronted with a lot of muddy and soft ground. I called the operator aside and more or less pleaded for some advice. I said I don't know what to do—you have seen situations like this before—what has worked in the past for you?

"He finally told me his idea. We tried it and, shazzam, it worked! We were quite successful. I thanked him for his advice and praised him for helping to solve the problem. Subsequently, he has been much more willing to contribute to team effort."

The lesson I learned is that it pays to be persistent when applying leadership principals such as letting it be their idea. The action I call you to is: Get the ideas from your team members and put them into use. The benefit you will gain is that your problems will be solved and your team members will feel more self assured.

A Dancing Team

Bob had been given the responsibility of planning an annual Western Square Dance Jubilee for his square-dancing club. This involved coordinating many different committees. At their follow-up meeting after this year's Jubilee, Bob wanted a positive planning session for next year, not a finger-pointing session. He did something that had never been done before. He brought an easel into the conference room and asked everyone for ideas to make next year's jubilee more successful. He wrote down the different positions and everything that was involved in planning next year's jubilee. He asked his fellow committee members to commit themselves to developing a checklist for their jobs by the end of the session.

Bob did not know how people would react to the idea of checklists and accountability in a volunteer group. To his surprise, they gave him all of the job descriptions and check lists he knew they needed by the end of the meeting. By empowering them—letting it be their idea—he gained their full cooperation. Next year's jubilee will be better than ever.

Railroaded

Vim was elected (or should I say, railroaded?) into the presidency of his Scandinavian Club while he was on vacation and not in attendance at the meeting. Partly because the club is made up of people older than himself, he found it difficult to implement any new ideas, and even though attendance and interest was waning on the part of many members and new members were not being brought in at the rate old members are literally dying off, Vim found it difficult to get his new ideas and suggestions into action. No matter what he suggested it seemed to be shot down. No matter what idea he brought to the group, they always had a good reason why it wouldn't work. Then, Vim tried a new strategy. His new strategy was to ask the group what they thought would work, how they thought they could increase membership, stimulate interest, have better more interesting programs and generally provide the services the club was originally designed to provide. Astoundingly, they had great ideas, many of which were the very ones that Vim had been hoping to see someone implement. They not only thought they were great ideas, they've been acting on these new ideas, and, from last reports, their club has more and happier members now than for a long time. So, if you want to get your ideas across, stop trying to come up with all the ideas, ask the other person what their ideas are.

To arouse peoples enthusiasm for your plans, include them in the planning process. If possible, arrange for them to begin by doing something which will be easy for them, yet which they will regard as a real achievement. Let it be their idea.

Whenever possible, an empowering leader tries to let plans come from the team and adopts and acts on the team's idea rather than their own.

Keep an eye on your ego. Few things are of greater handicap in working with others and building a winning team than an exaggerated idea of your own ability and importance. Empowering leaders are big enough not to compete for personal credit with their own team members. Real leaders want their team members to standout. They know that when their team looks good, they do too. They really understand that the only way they can look good is when their team looks good.

So surround yourself with people who are better than you, and then let it be their idea.

> *"The best ideas are common property."*
> Lucius Anaeus Seneca

Respirators

Phil, the president of an industrial commercial paint contracting company, told our Leadership Development Lab:

"We are using Xylene-based paint products on some of our new projects. The paint is highly toxic, and to protect our crew, we need for all of them to wear a high test respirator. We have been in the habit of wearing respirators for years, but the over-cup we have used was not working since it did not filter out the toxic fumes of the Xylene-based paint. This was a very undesirable, potentially dangerous situation.

"I went into action, and, after looking around on my own, I bought a new, improved type of respirator which I thought was a much better answer to meet our requirements. The new respirators were perfect technically, and no fumes got through, but didn't work out well because these were not at all comfortable, so the crew just would not wear them. So, from a practical point of view they did not meet our needs.

"After spending $500 on respirators I thought would solve our problem, I was no closer to a solution than when I started. I finally decided to ask our crew, the people who actually used the respirators on a daily basis, for their input. We talked about all the different types of respirators that are available. We discussed their strengths and potential weaknesses. After a thorough discussion, getting everyone's ideas, points of view and input,we all agreed on a direction, and made a decision."

The lesson I learned is that a majority of those who are involved in the use of a product are the ones who should be included in the decision of what product to use. It just makes sense, and it demonstrates the value of letting it be their idea.

Suggestions

The Japanese know the value of encouraging idea development—of letting it be his idea. It is one explanation for why Japan is a tough industrial competitor: Two out of three Japanese employees submit suggestions to save money, increase efficiency and boost morale, as compared to only eight percent of American workers. The Japanese average 2,472 suggestions per 100 eligible employees. The average suggestions from U.S. employees is 13 per 100. Toyota gets five times as many employee suggestions as GM. Its U.S. market share is rising; GM's is falling. Coincidence? Data from a 1987 report by the National Association of Suggestion Systems indicate that Japanese employers adopt four of five suggestions. Their U.S.counterparts adopt one of four. Another factor is that in Japan small suggestions are encouraged, while in the United States, companies favor suggestions that go for the "home run." New Japanese employees are expected to contribute four suggestions per workday the first few months of their employment. American companies grant an average award of $604.72 per suggestion utilized, as opposed to Japan's average payment of $3.23. However, net savings resulting from employee suggestion per 100 employees is $274,475 in Japan versus $24,891 in the U.S.

Brain Storming

You can introduce brainstorming as a technique to get members of your team to come up with ideas that help the organization. This was put into action by Brad who told our Leadership Development Lab:

"We have eight trucks and it seems like we are not using them as best we could—too much overtime, late deliveries, poor attitudes. I decided to buy a flip chart and use a green light brainstorming session. I explained the problem as I saw it (everyone agreed) and said for two minutes I wanted them to throw out any ideas they might have to improve our truck use.

"In just two minutes I got 15 ideas three of which we can put in use immediately. These solutions were very simple, and will probably save at least 10 hours per week per branch. The best part was that when I asked for their help, I got it and everybody left the meeting with a renewed sense of commitment to their jobs."

The lesson I learned is when I have a problem, use the

brainstorming technique to get everyone involved with the solution. The action I call you to is: Use the green light brainstorming technique whenever you are facing a problem that involves all or several members of your team. The benefit you gain is that everyone will "buy" into the plan if they are part of the problem solving. This creates a fantastic team atmosphere and anything is possible.

B. Y. O. S. S.

I asked several members of our team to come into my office. There were five of us. I wanted to develop a flyer we can mail to our friends inviting them to an end-of-the-summer yard and pool party and announce upcoming fall events for Turbo Management Systems. "First, let's decide when." Someone left the room and brought in our planning calendar. "Now, what will we say to get attention?" Someone said, "Back to the future." "How about flashback?" "How about flashback splash?" "Great! Flashback splash." "Great! Let's make it B.Y.O.S.S." "What's B.Y.O.S.S.?" "Bring Your Own Success Story." "Fabulous!" And on it went.

We developed a far better flyer in less than 20 minutes than I or any of us working alone could have developed in days. What I learned from this experience is the power of synergism—creative, positive, directed brainstorming. With synergism, the whole is greater than the sum of the parts. Two positive heads are better than one. With synergism, two plus two equals eight or 64 or some multiplier that's off the scale. I was also reminded of the feeling of worth, belonging, contribution, and value I gain from participating with others in creative effort.

Today, stop for a moment, regardless of your position. Get your customers or suppliers or coworkers, subordinates or family together, and have a brainstorming session, a directed, creative thinking session. You'll create synergistic power that will allow you to solve problems quickly with relative ease. More importantly, you will feel better about yourself, you will empower them, and they will empower you.

Dr. J. P. Guilford of the University of Southern California says that creativity—the quality needed to become an innovator—can be deliberately developed. One way is to remove the "mental blocks" that stand in the way of ideas. The most important mental blocks are:

1. Unawareness of the fact that each of us is gifted with creative potential.

2. Failure to realize that all of us can do much to make ourselves more creative.

3. Unwillingness to try and to keep trying to think up new and better ideas.

The biggest mental blocks are those movies in the mind that play on our fear of rejection or failure. One antidote to fear is the energy derived from brainstorming.

How To Brainstorm

Two heads are better than one! When you have a complex problem to solve or a new campaign to design, gather several minds and brainstorm your way to innovative and creative success!

Getting a group of people with diverse ideas and perceptions to brainstorm effectively takes more than simply popping them down into chairs in the same room and expecting a miracle. Productive brainstorming takes organization. Because the creativity inside each person is best unleashed in a relaxed atmosphere, I believe you might want to throw a brainstorming "party" to put people in a positive frame of mind right from the start.

Brainstorming is a process by which people generate as many ideas as possible without evaluation by others. The key to brainstorming is the separation of idea generation and evaluation or judging the ideas that are generated.

There has been a lot of research on creativity and problem solving. All of this research has supported the idea that the process of brainstorming leads to greater creativity, better solutions to problems, and commitment on the part of the group.

Brainstorming can be done in several ways:

Freewheeling

In the "freewheeling," or letting ideas flow method, everyone contributes ideas spontaneously. This method encourages creativity as people build on each other's ideas. The disadvantage is that quieter members of the group often do not speak up. You may miss some people's ideas.

Taking Turns

In a taking turns process, people present their ideas one at a time in sequence. The advantage of this method is that everybody gets equal time to speak up and quieter people are more likely to contribute. The disadvantage is that it stifles spontaneity and sometimes members forget their idea by the time their turn arrives. In this process, members should be allowed to "pass" if they have no suggestions.

Paper Pass

In this method everyone puts ideas on a slip of paper and passes them in to the leader or facilitator. The advantage of this method is that some people may be more candid and creative with their anonymity preserved. The disadvantage is in not hearing other member's ideas which often trigger add-on creativity.

It is best to choose the style most comfortable for your team or do some combination of the three methods.

Try these ten tips for organizing and coaching a successful creative team:

- Create a climate in which all team members feel free to communicate openly—the resource party. Loosen up with team-building exercises, such as work games, that open the mind. Games help break interpersonal barriers, and they get everyone on your team actively listening and involved.
- Present your ideas to the team with conviction, confidence and enthusiasm.
- Prepare a written agenda to hand out and preview with the entire team.
- Ask questions that involve everyone, and never allow one person to monopolize the discussion. Phrase questions in ways that will arouse emotional responses and elicit hidden ideas from even the quietest members of the group.
- Offer positive feedback to individuals regarding their contributions to the team. Do this objectively and often.
- Acknowledge individuals by name when listening to their ideas.
- Don't worry about semantics; worry about being understood. Encourage people to say what they mean. For example, instead of sliding around the rainbow of color choices, get right to the point with "Let's use red!"
- Monitor non-verbal communication. Body language can tell a great deal about the team's progress. Watch for people stiffening up and crossing their arms and legs a though defending against attack.

- Provide interim summaries. This gives people the encouragement of hearing their own ideas again.
- Acknowledge the team's shared accomplishments, and make sure that team members are aware of the impact of their ideas on solving the initial problem. Give credit to the entire group, even after the brainstorming session.

One good way to brainstorm is to apply the idea-spurring questions developed by Dr. Alex Osborn, in his book, *Applied Imagination*. By the time you have made the following four sets of questions a habit—you will have already doubled your idea output.

1. Are there other uses for your idea or product?

    "Is there a new way to use it as it is?" (like three-wheel motorcycle as a farm implement)

    "Are there other ways it can be used if modified?" (like a cover so you can use it in the rain)

    "What could be made from this?" (like ground up dollars made into 'million dollar' paper-weights)

    "How about salvaging?" (like turning o-nuts, washers and spark-plugs into art)

2. Adapt?

    "What else is like this?" (like a supercharged airplane is like a turbocharged car)

    "What parallels does the past provide?" (like the supercharger on the Auburn in 1937)

    "Could other processes be copied?" (hanging cars on a conveyor belt like beef to make a production line)

    "What other ideas might be adaptable?" (like Diesel who got his engine ideas from a cigar lighter)

3. Modify?

    "What other shape can we try?" (like the buggy maker who tapered the roller bearing which Leonardo da Vinci had invented 400 years before)

"What other forms can we try?" (like bath gel instead of bar soap)

"How can we create a new look?" (like a wedge-shaped car)

"What could color do?" (like pink and other pastels in automobiles to make 1955 one of the biggest new-car years in history)

"How about motion?" (like seat belts that automatically lock)

"What about sound?" (like the rotary engine that "hums" instead of going "ping, ping")

4. Magnify?

"Should we provide for a longer time?" (like a 50,000-mile warranty)

"Should we offer with greater frequency?" (like changing oil every 2,500 miles in a diesel to prolong life and cut maintenance costs)

"Should we increase strength?" (like reinforced heels and toes in hosiery)

"What about height?" (like high boy 4 x 4 pickup trucks)

You build an empowered team when you use every idea you possibly can from team members.

o   o   o

Utilize Their Ideas

Risk Taking Is Free

To laugh is to risk appearing the fool.
To weep is to risk appearing sentimental.
To reach out for another is to risk involvement.
To expose feeling is to risk exposing your true self.
To place your ideas, your dreams before the
crowd is to risk their loss.
To love is to risk not being loved in return.
To live is to risk dying.
To hope is to risk despair.
To try is to risk failure.
But the risk must be taken, because the greatest
hazard in life is to risk nothing.
The person who risks nothing, does nothing, has
nothing and is nothing.
He may avoid suffering and sorrow, but he simply
cannot learn, feel, change, grow, love, live.
Chained by his certitudes, he is a slave, he has
forfeited freedom.
Only a person who risks—is free.

Author Unknown

>>>12

Dramatize Your Idea

"Do nothing ordinary."
Ralph Waldo Emerson

This is a time for drama. Merely stating a truth is not enough. When we talk about important matters and need to sell our ideas, we must be more vivid and interesting ... yes, even dramatic. "Showmanship" —that's the ticket! The movies do it, television does it. So can you. Be creative! Arouse curiosity. Be unexpected and dramatic. You can do this by combining something "new" with what is already familiar.

Red Sweater

John, president of the Portland Cement Company is said to have gotten his start by using showmanship when he was a clerk at Armour's packing plant. Knowing that Mr. Armour had a habit of coming down to the plant very early in the morning, he came in early himself. Instead of the usual business clothes of the other clerks, he wore a red sweater. One day Mr. Armour inquired, "Who is that?" John caught the boss's attention—he was singled out from among all the other clerks. Now he had a chance to demonstrate his abilities. That was all he needed to focus the boss's attention so he could see for himself what an outstanding job John was doing.

Hug

Mac told our Leadership Development Lab that he went into his secretary's office and asked her to stand up and put her arms around him to give him a hug, so she did. Then she asked what this was all about. Mac told her she was his "pearl," the person he picked during the Lab to improve his relationship with. She thought that was great. Mac gave her a little plant with a small bear on it to remind her of him. Then Mac told her he really enjoyed working with her and expressed his thanks for her being his pearl. They sat down and talked things out so they understood each other's problems. It works!

The lesson Mac learned is to put heart-felt feeling with dramatics into his communication. The benefits you will gain when you risk being dramatically different are better relationships and that adds up to improved working conditions.

Everyone Loves A Parade

On Saturday morning, at about 7:00, we joined the overnight campers and the other early risers in anticipation on one of the nation's greatest displays of flowers, bands, and humanity—ultimately 500,000 of us united to celebrate life, living and being together—a parade. Everyone loves a parade. We were there to sell souvenir programs as a fund-raiser for our church. I loved the fun of interacting with the crowd. We worked hawking the programs for four hours before the parade began. Some people were camped out and waited for over 12 hours. Oh, how we love a parade! My favorite part of the parade is the One-More-Time-Around band. The average age must be 40 and they are all former high school and college band members who love to get together once a year for the Rose Parade. They are so exuberant and so full of life!

Since we all love a parade the action I call you to is to provide the added value to your life today by putting out a little something extra—the music to march to, the smile of a clown, the beauty of a princess. Like Donald Trump and his yachts and hotels, Liberache and his candelabra, and Malcolm Forbes with his motorcycles, grip the other person's attention by doing something unexpected. These people understood showmanship. They used what was "new" and different to astonish the other person and to arouse his curiosity. Gaining people's attention by expressing your views and perspectives in a novel and interesting way, breaking their preoccupation, can be a powerful leadership tool.

Don't Wait To Be Great

I can't wait to tell you about my great day, yesterday. I stopped by Thomas Joseph's Personalized Dry Cleaning in Greenhouse Square, Clackamas, Oregon. When I called Thomas from my car about 4:48, I was near Southgate. Thomas told me how to drive straight to his gate. Seriously. Joseph is passionate about his dry cleaning business. He's been featured in newspaper articles, photographed with Blazers and Senators. He's been honored by his Rotary club. As he showed me around his business, once again I was reminded that excellence, joy, passion and verve, excitement and fun are where you find them.

I first spotted Joseph carrying dry cleaning out to one of his customer's cars. I watched him as he greeted every customer by name as they walked into his store. Now wait 'till you read what he did with the announcement of his eighth birthday:

> Let's celebrate! For **8** great years, you've depended on Thomas Joseph for his personalized dry cleaning services, and to celebrate the **8**th anniversary of Thomas Joseph's Dry Cleaning service, Thomas wants to say "Thank you in **8** great ways for **8** years of wonderful customers, with a special birthday party— Thursday **8/8** and Friday **8/9** from **8**:00 to **8**:00 come in for great cake and coffee. We can't wait to see you.

And on and on and on he went, with eight ways, eight specials. All of which, of course, feature the numeral eight. Where did all of this creativity and innovation come from? It came from his team, as he likes to refer to the 16 people who work for him. Thomas sat down with his team and they brainstormed all of the great ways to play up the significance of the figure eight. What a neat piece of showmanship and dramatization of an idea. Why wait to be great? Sit up straight, mate. There's greatness inside of you. Take the bait. Look for and find eight ways to be great. It's not too late. You've got a date with fate.

Party Time

Yesterday morning, we completed 72 weeks of training for what has been our key client for the past year and a half. After completing the formal session, we had a graduation. I didn't know we could have so much fun—balloons, whistles, poppers, pictures and cake. How do you view celebration? Webster

says that celebration is "to honor publicly, to extol, to com-
memorate, with ceremony or festival, to have a congenial time,
to break with normal business." A Chinese proverb says,
"Ceremony is the smoke of friendship."

Think right now of one of your birthdays. If you're as
old as I am, you have several to review. Which one do you
remember? For most of us, it's one we've celebrated with
bravado, gusto. With celebration, we create bonding. When we
celebrate accomplishments and achievements, we anchor them,
we can establish them as new norms. We really get a sense of
our accomplishments. We see them as worthwhile. When we
celebrate a right, we acknowledge ourselves, we empower ourselves and others as winners and achievers. This builds self-
esteem, team, and esprit-de-corps, and we can ready ourselves
to win again.

Today, find a reason to celebrate. If you can't find a reason to celebrate, make one. Your celebration will serve as a
turbo thrust to new altitudes of achievement.

Green Wallpaper

A lot can happen in sales when a leader decides to do
something out of the ordinary. Steve told me this fantastic story:

As the VP of sales and marketing for a salad dressing,
pancake syrup, shortening and oil company, one of the necessary evils of my job is attending each year the annual food
shows and mini food shows. This is where the manufacturers
are held up for $800 or more for a booth to exhibit their prod-
ucts. These shows have become profit centers for some distrib-
utors. They give away great vacations, cars, and prizes under
their name but with the manufacturer's money. Oh yeah, they
also expect you to have greatly reduced prices with a buy in, as
well as Spiff money for the customer and or the sales people. It

really is good for everyone except for the manufacturer. The shows can stimulate sales at the expense of profits.

After my first several shows as a manufacturer I was really feeling like a sucker. Until I hit on an idea to sell lots of products with a twist on the Spiff money.

I ordered 100 sheets of uncut $1.00 dollar bills from the Federal Mint. I bought some tape, a rod and some plexiglass. Our booth was wall to wall money. We had a small sample table in front and bulk commodities visible in back. As people came by they would point at the sheets of money in the plexiglas and ask, "Is this real?" "What are you selling?" "How much do I need to buy to get a half sheet of greenbacks?" By the end of the show my salesman and I had sold over five and one half trucks of merchandise. People were carrying around our uncut bills almost like an advertising banner, and talking about us and our booth. When we took a break, we went to the restaurant across the street known for good food. With the other brokers and manufacturers we sat at the bar waiting for a table. When we were called I presented the payment to the bartender. He took it to the cash register and promptly came back, and said, "This is about the twentieth time I have got this stuff tonight. Who is selling the money? It is illegal."

So I explained that the money was real and basically anyone can buy it from the U.S. Mint in sheets. It is illegal to deface or cut into the green part of a bill.

The next year at the same show this lady and her husband who had previously bought twelve sheets worth of product came back to the show. I saw her come in. She made a beeline to my booth from the front door. "How much do I need to buy to get nineteen sheets of money?" "Nineteen sheets!" I said, "You bought twelve sheets last year. Why do you want nineteen sheets?" She said, "We papered our bathroom wall with the first twelve and we figure we need nineteen more to finish!"

Expensive wallpaper.

The upshot of all this was that we won the best sales award at most of our shows this year, as well as the single booth award for unique idea.

Part of dramatizing your idea is to look at your organization to discover the persons in it who have unusual ways of thinking or who display curiosity as part of their insatiable thirst for answers to the question of how things work and what could be done to make them work better.

In his newspaper column, management excellence, Tom Peters chose curious people as a theme and some of his comments are valuable for us to think about:

The question: How do you and I, as independent contributors on or off someone's payroll, stay curious? And how do chiefs keep organizations imaginative?

• Hire curious people. How can you tell if people are curious? Easy. They've consistently avoided the mainstream: took a year off without pay to work in the inner city; keep bees as a lifelong hobby; set aside six weeks each year to travel abroad. If curiosity isn't on a person's resume, don't expect it to bloom tomorrow in your business.

The corollary is obvious: Don't hire incurious people. If they boast the solid gold resume (right school, right grades, right first job, and right year for first promotion), watch out—honest!

• Hire a few genuine off-the-wall sorts—i.e., collect weirdos. In addition to seeking curious people in general, try to implant a few real head cases into your joint from time to time. Bankroll them until they can invent a wacky project that will spark the whole organization.

• "Measure" curiosity. It's time for semi-annual performance reviews. Consider having each employee submit a one-page essay on: (a) the oddest thing I've done this year off the job,

(b) the craziest idea I've tried at work, or (c) my most original screw-up, on the job or off. Using the answers to such questions, deal curiosity directly into the evaluation deck, near the top.

• Seek out curious work. At Britain's Imagination (a marketing consultancy, more or less), founder Gary Withers, dubbed Britain's Walt Disney by some pundits, says he won't take assignments that don't provide an opportunity to out-do the firm's zaniest prior performance. Beware of taking on the big, prestigious job assignment that is as dull as can be.

• Change pace. Go to work next Thursday and declare it miniature-golf day. Hey, why not? Showing a training film this afternoon? Order popcorn for every participant.

Interesting ideas, eh?

Oakland "A"s

Change pace is what our daughter-in-law, Juliana Dennis did when she announced to her thirty department managers that she had arranged a visit to the company's distribution center and they should wear their jeans and sneakers.

She asked the managers to meet her at 10 A.M. at her Walnut Creek store where a chartered bus would be waiting to pick up everybody. When the bus started of in the direction of Oakland, California instead of the distribution center the managers became suspicious. Their suspicions turned to joy and surprise when the bus took them to the Oakland Stadium where the Oakland "A"s were playing a baseball game.

Juliana had arranged box seats for her team of managers who ate hot dogs and drank cokes and had an unscheduled vacation day at company expense.

This is how you build collective loyalty and job enthusiasm. Give your team a surprise and you will be surprised by the renewed commitment the team members bring back to their jobs after you've demonstrated that you care enough to do something special for them.

Stimulate Competition

A great way to get things done and enhance jobs is to stimulate competition. Money alone does not bring good people together, nor does it hold them together. Exciting ideas do! It is the game itself, the competition to excel, the chance to prove their worth, and the opportunity to win that bring and hold a team together. That's what makes foot races, hog calling contests, and pie eating contests—the desire to excel and the desire for a feeling of importance.

Well, there is another way you can help your organization to become more effective, to become more than ordinary, and that is by increasing the challenge, but not the workload. This was put in perspective for me by Sharon who told our Leadership Development Lab:

New Accounts Count

"Tom, my supervisor, and I had been talking about the morale in our office and began brainstorming ideas to "spark" our office staff's enthusiasm. I suggested we try a new and different incentive for them.

"We wanted them to get out and see what the salesmen and drivers are faced with every day as they make sales and service calls, so we derived a retail sales incentive program for them. After deciding on the specifics of the incentive program, Tom and I presented it to the general manager, who approved it heartily.

"I told the office staff my ideas, and we formed teams to

go out to present our products and small-store promotions to small retail accounts that were not presently buying our products. Maxine and I went out first because I had some sure buys to get the team's adrenaline going and bolster their belief that we could do it.

"When we came back with four placements the first day, everyone was really excited. As each team went out on sales calls, the excitement grew and the challenge to win the competition grew. After two weeks, we had placed 35 new products in previously inactive accounts.

"The whole company was buzzing about our successes, and our inside office team was elated—morale was at an all-time high. Tom and I shot down the obstacles to make our goal a reality. We still laugh about how scared we were and about our unprofessional sales pitches!"

The lesson we can learn from Sharon's vignette is: The way to build the morale of our team, the way we help them to be more than ordinary, is not to lessen the challenge or add more work, but, instead, to add more opportunity and diversity to the job challenges we face. This is sometimes called "job enhancement," and it is always empowering.

Star

I was conducting a workshop for Boise Cascade the other day at the Red Lion Inn. A young waiter came into the room during one of the breaks with a tub of pop and set it in the middle of the table. When I looked at him, I noticed on his name tag a little blue stick-on star (the kind you might get at Sunday school), and it wasn't on straight—it was a little off center. Howard, "I asked, "what is the blue star for?

He answered. "Oh, the star? We're having a safety contest. We're trying to see who can be the safest hare. We're in teams, and my team was the safest last month. That's why I got a blue star. And, if we win, we get an award.

I said, "What is the award if you win?"

He replied, "I don't know, but I think it's a pizza."

Howard wasn't sure what the award was going to be, but he was motivated by the outcome, the CONTEST.

Now, my challenge to you is: Find a way, today, to lessen the boredom your team faces when all they do is the routine, menial tasks. Give your team new creative challenges to meet. Help them to rise above the level of ordinariness. Up the challenge (not the workload) for them—the challenge that allows for personal growth. This challenge will motivate your team members as they find ways to create solutions to troubling problems.

Find a way to enrich the work of your team by building in a contest. And be sure there are some ways to have immediate wins. When the wins come, celebrate your successes. Celebration provides the afterburner effect that will turbocharge your team.

CUZ

The subject of stimulating competition came up not long ago when Duane told our Leadership Development Lab:

"At our September 1992 managers' meeting, we brainstormed the question, 'In what ways can we improve customer service?' We developed a multiplicity of ideas and ultimately landed on a program we decided to call CUZ (Customer U-awareness Zone). Our goals were to improve customer awareness, in-house customer service and, ultimately, sales.

"We defined the Customer U-awareness Zone as the 10-foot radius around a customer. The goal was to ensure that all customer service personnel, stockers and managers at G.I. Joe's said, 'Hello,' acknowledged, paid attention to and, as appropriate, asked to help customers. Any time anyone was within 10 feet of a customer we were within the CUZ and we needed to greet the customer.

"To help ensure our store management was completely on board and leading by example, we challenged the store managers and assistant manager. When and if one of our employees caught them (management) not living up to the CUZ zone by failing to greet a customer within 10 feet, the employee was instructed to tap the manager or assistant on the shoulder and say, 'CUZ.'

"Each manager was given a stock of CUZ slips. Each CUZ slip was worth 50 cents toward a Halloween surprise at our annual fall Halloween luncheon. At the end of the month, each store manager reported at our managers' meeting the number of times they had been caught and the number of their slips they had given out. The goal, of course, was to see how few times they were caught and how few of their CUZ slips they had given out.

"As of now, the leading store has given out only six CUZ slips. What this has done for our customer service awareness has been almost unbelievable, and, in terms of increased sales, we have just completed the best fall season in the history of our firm. We have actually had customers asking if our employees are on a commission.

"The lesson I learned is that by throwing down a challenge, introducing a little friendly, fun competition, people will change their behavior. Friendly, fun competition can go a long way toward creating enhanced esprit de corps, greater customer awareness and, in our case, increased sales and profits."

The action I ask you to take is: Give your group, your company, your team, a little friendly competition aimed at improving customer response time, customer awareness or quality. Find a way to throw down a challenge to management. Reverse roles; let the team catch the boss for a change.

The benefit you will gain is the natural response of extended effort because everyone wants to win. The level of excellence to which you are challenging them will raise. You may have your best year ever.

o   o   o

Dramatize Your Ideas
Stimulate Competition

"People seldom learn from the mistakes of others—
Not because they deny the value of the past,
But because they are faced with new problems."

Ilya Ehrenburg

"The man who can own up to his own error
Is greater than he who merely knows how to avoid making it."

Cardinal DeRetz

"A life spent in making mistakes
Is not only more honorable
But more useful than a life spent doing nothing."

George Bernard Shaw

>>>13

Myth Of Miss-Takes

"Experience is the name everyone gives to their mistakes."
Oscar Wilde

The myth of mistakes. If we create a culture that does not allow for mistakes, doesn't permit people to err, which is overly harsh when people stumble, we create a culture which will be masterful at coverup and people will become skillful at pointing at and blaming others. A culture that takes no risks, no chances, is a culture where little improvement occurs.

Blueprints

Dave told our Leadership Development Lab a great story about going out to a new job assignment. He took his set of blueprints. When he arrived at the job site and opened up the prints to begin to familiarize himself with the project the most important blueprint was missing.

He called back to his office. "Where is the main project print?" he asked. His office called the project design people.

"Where is the blue print?"

"Nothing here. You have it."

"No, you have it!"

A day later, still no blueprint. Three days later, still no blueprint. Everything was up in the air. Dave kept calling them and saying, "It's going to be hard to do this job right without *all* the blueprints."

On the fourth day, Dave was looking through some of his drawings, and there, to his amazement, was the missing blueprint. He had the print all the time!

Wow, was he embarrassed! What to do? Well, we know the right answer: Call the office immediately and admit the mistake. We also know the other possible answers: Hide it; throw it away; sneak it back to the office so it looks like it was always there. Boy, can we be creative when it comes to covering up our mistakes? But if we wish to create an empowered organization, we must allow people the space to be honest. Allow people the space to admit their faults and errors so that we can have empowered teams. To Dave's credit that's what Dave did. He called his office and admitted that he had had the print the whole time—and *he* had misplaced it.

As empowering leaders, what should our attitude be toward mistakes? First, let's break the work down: Mis-takes—like in the movie business. Our son owns a video production business, Chase Teleproductions. When he is shooting a commercial or a training video and the first TAKE isn't successful, he shoots a second take, a third take and so on. There is no blame, shame or attempt to shift responsibility. We know that high-performance companies have a similar attitude toward mistakes. They have learned that they must allow for, and even encourage, mistakes—especially mistakes that are inevitable while in the pursuit of a better way, a new way, an improved way. Unless there is an atmosphere that allows for mistakes, there will be no risk-taking and we may even create an atmosphere where people abandon the commitment to honesty. Continuous improvement will be replaced by complacency and adherence to policies and procedures. The driving force will be: Play it safe.

The action I call you to is: When *you* blow it, show it. When *you* make a mistake, be willing to admit it, and allow your team to do the same. This is how you will create empowered teams and, at the same time, strengthen your own self-esteem.

Broken Panes

Kelly told our Leadership Development Lab that after going to work as a glass installer he was assigned the job of placing windows in the remodel of the Montgomery Park Building in Portland, Oregon. As he was moving the long, heavy boxes up the scaffolding to work on top of the structure four stories in the air he heard the gut-wrenching sound of glass breaking. He struggled to get in control of the falling boxes—too late. Eleven windows were broken—a loss of material and time—potentially creating a scheduling bottleneck. When Kelly reluctantly called the office to relate what had happened, he was told after a little bit of laughter that accidents happen. "Don't worry about it, just keep moving. We have some extra windows already available."

The lesson I learned from that example is that capable leaders are prepared for the inevitable breakdowns that occur as we're moving toward our objectives, moving toward our goals. They do not over dramatize the mistakes. They expect a few mistakes along the way. The action I call you to is this: Make allowances for reasonable errors in judgment and performance. The benefit you'll gain is a smooth-running, high-performance, empowered team.

Pilings

Dee, a senior project engineer, told our Leadership Development Lab a marvelous story. He spent a number of hours and a great deal of effort laying out a project plan for one of his young, self-assured project engineers. Dee went over the plan in great detail with the new assistant project manager, and when they were done, Dee felt he had eliminated any possibility for misunderstanding. The project engineer went to the job site and began work.

After the project had been in progress for a couple of days, the owner's survey crew showed up to inspect the project. They discovered that the entire structure, a drydock, was nine feet from where the plans specified.

The owner's representative called Dee. "It looks to us like your crew has set the pilings for the mooring nine feet from where the plans specify." Dee jumped into his pickup and rushed over to take a look at the project. Sure enough, the structure was in the wrong place.

"I was biting my tongue," Dee said. "I wanted to say, 'How could you be so stupid? How could you make a mistake like this?'"

Dee told us that just a few short years ago, he had fired someone on the spot for this kind of mistake. This time, though, he and this young project engineer went to work on a modified plan to make things work.

And, as is often the case in this kind of situation, they were able to find a way that did work—a plan that made the owner happy and ended up not costing any additional money or time.

Dee left the job site, and when he returned a day later, he

found that there was a lot of kidding going on. When the project engineer would go over to get the pickup truck, somebody would say, "Better be careful with that. If you drive nine feet too far to the left, you'll end up in the river." Dee encouraged the crew to lighten up.

He said that his project engineer was working harder than ever, had a good attitude, and was putting his heart and head into the job.

"Had I lost my temper and fired this guy, it would have been a far bigger mistake than the project engineer's mistake of putting the pilings in the wrong place," Dee said. "His mistake cost a little time and credibility. If I had made the mistake of firing him, it would have cost our firm a great deal in lost time, lost training and experience."

Dee added: "The lesson I learned is that if my intention is to build people and make them successful, I don't need to rub it in when they've made a mistake. I don't need to jam the beans up the nose or rub salt into the wound. What I need to do is help them save face, learn from their experience and move on."

Dee said that he has more power when he withholds judgment, criticism and condemnation than he can ever gain by attacking the mistakes his team makes.

So, this week, when your team makes a mistake, make it an opportunity to build champions.

Admit It

A few weeks ago, I watched a young man stand in front of our Leadership Development Lab and talk about the frustrating relationship he has with his ex-wife. He hadn't wanted the divorce in the first place, and they were becoming more and more distant all the time. Finally, as a result of the stimulation of the class, he asked his ex-wife if they could talk about what was causing the distance between them

She said, "You've never admitted you were wrong."

As he was telling this story to the class, he had a very difficult time saying, "I admitted I was wrong." In fact, he couldn't say, "I admitted I was wrong," until I asked him to say those exact words—"I admitted I was wrong." When he said the words, his face changed. His brow was smooth, his eyes were open and a smile came over his face. I watched this young man, who was hiding behind pride and fear begin to experience the power and confidence, the release that comes when we we simply say, "I'm wrong."

When you make mistakes—mistakes in performance, mistakes in the way you interact with people—be courageous enough to admit that you were wrong in the way you handled the situation. Take full responsibility for every decision you make. Never blame others for something that goes wrong that is really your responsibility. Be willing to say, "I was wrong." Taking this approach will set the example for others to be as courageous, as humble, as trainable, as realistic, as coachable as you. We can waste a lot of time and energy trying to cover up our mistakes, goofs and errors. When we willingly admit errors in judgment, action and performance, we win respect. Admitting our mistakes relieves tension and moves us up many notches in the eyes of our team members, friends and loved ones. It also establishes a model for appropriate professional behavior for others to follow.

Up To Your Neck In It

There are advantages to being honest about mistakes that are not immediately evident. Mark tells a story that demonstrates this. He was an area coordinator for a paper machine trial which was testing a vendor's new additives. The vendor told Mark that they might be running out of his additive and be forced to shut down the trial. Mark went to investigate. While standing on a platform above a tank containing the additive, he noticed the additive was running low. As he was leaning over with the tape measure trying to get an accurate measurement of the supply remaining, the platform collapsed and he fell into the tank, which contained about four feet of slurry. Mark makes a strong point for safety by using his own example of blowing it.

My Wife Was Right

A remarkably good example of how to admit a mistake, on error in judgement, was demonstrated by Tom Peterson, a Portland-area retailer, who recently filed for bankruptcy. He bought a company called Stereo Super Stores against his wife's advice and his decision was disastrous. He ran a full page advertisement in the Oregonian:

I'm in trouble.
I have been forced to take Chapter 11
reorganization in the Courts.
I made a mistake.
I should have listened to my wife.
She said, "Don't buy Stereo Super Stores;
it won't work." She was right.
I've been successful before.
I can be successful again,
But I'll need your help.
Whatever you need in TVs, Stereos,
Furniture and Appliances, please buy today.
Our prices have always been right;
they're even better now!
I promise you the same friendly
customer service you deserve and expect.

*My family and I want to extend
our personal thanks to the hundreds
of customers who responded last week.*
Now, Peterson's action was a remarkable example of
turning disaster into a positive asset.

Overdrawn

In another case, the comptroller of a construction firm in
Seattle told us that as he was balancing his accounts, he discovered to his astonishment that the company was overdrawn. They
have a credit line, but they don't like to tap into it. He felt he had
no choice but to immediately go into the president's office and
tell him what he'd done. He and the president then called the
bank, and they all began to research their account. I know we all
love a story with a happy ending, and this has one. As it turns out
the bank had make a mistake; they had blown it. See what a
much stronger position the comptroller was in having admitted
immediately, versus running around, trying to cover it up, trying
to solve the problem on his own? "When You Blow It, Show It"
not only in the long term helps you save face with others, but it
helps you save a tremendous amount of personal stress and
enables you to maintain your enthusiasm and integrity with others.

Of all the principles of leadership, perhaps one of the
most difficult to follow is the willingness of the team's leader, to
admit it when he's wrong.

Honesty about mistakes almost always results in praise
from the person we tell about them. Carolyn told us a story
about her frustrated boss bringing some work into her office
which he thought one of Carolyn's people had done and in a dis-
gusted way threw it on her desk. "Would you please tell so-and-
so that this is not the form in which I'd like to have my work

done in the future," he said.

He left the office. Carolyn looked at what he'd put on her desk and realized it was work that she had done. She was then faced with a decision—a decision not unlike the decisions you and I are faced with from time to time, a decision which tests our character, a decision which will significantly impact the team. Carolyn looked at the work, went through a few minutes of decision making, picked it up, walked to her boss's office and said, "I'm sorry, I need to tell you that I'm the one who did this work, not the other party."

Of course her boss was surprised that she was forthright, honest, and we all can guess enough about the situation to figure out that Carolyn went a long way toward empowering her team and herself.

"We are not afraid...to tolerate any error
so long as reason is left free to combat it."
Thomas Jefferson

"Standing on your own dignity makes for poor footing.
Arnold Glasow

Resignation

Many people will be familiar with the Associated Press dispatch that was carried in newspapers all over the United States on August 8, 1974:

WASHINGTON (AP)—President Nixon resigned Thursday night, effective at noon Friday, telling the nation "America needs a full-time president and a full-time Congress" freed of the pressures of Watergate and impeachment.

Nixon, in his final address from the Oval Office of the White House, said he leaves without bitterness toward his foes, with thanks for those who have supported him through the months of Watergate disclosures and crises. He thus relinquished the White House to Vice President Gerald R. Ford, who is to take the oath of office at noon Friday.

"The leadership of America will be in good hands," Nixon said. Nixon, his face grim but his voice steady, said he was stepping aside in the national interest. His base of support in Congress, he said, had eroded to the point at which he would not have backing for the crucial decisions that confront the president.

In that situation, he said, the constitutional process that would have been served by impeachment has been fulfilled, and there is no longer a need to prolong the struggle.

Nixon said he would have preferred to fight to the end for the job he won in an historic landslide nearly two years ago.

" But the interest of the nation must always come before any personal consideration," Nixon said.

If you remember that day, then you'll also probably remember how you felt. I think many of us shared the regret that here was a man we had elected to the highest office in the land who couldn't admit that he was wrong; he couldn't admit that he had made a mistake and was unable to ask citizens to forgive his mischief. What do you think might have happened if he had been up front with the American people? Don't you think they would have supported him?

Whether it's the man in the White House, or your own team, the quality that helps build a championship team is a right attitude toward Mistakes. And that's all a mistake is just a mistake. It isn't something for us to pull our hair out about and get down and kick and scream about or a time for us to give up. A mistake is something that wasn't done correctly. It was a mistake. The right view of mistakes will allow us to say, "Okay, let's try it again." A culture that does not allow for mistakes will create people who will hide their mistakes, not stick their necks out, not take risks, and not take chances. They will play cover up. They'll point at other people. They won't say, "I blew it." And you can not move forward unless people are willing to quickly admit their mistakes. Henry Ford said, "Failure is the opportunity to begin again more intelligently."

How many of you think there's room for all of us to have a better, maybe a little lighter touch around mistakes or be a little more courageous in admitting our faults?" It's a major problem in many companies. Take risks, make *mistakes,* test limits. "Playing it safe" does not move the business forward. Letting go of power may increase it. Delegating may free us from routine and enrich the work of our people. Challenging outdated processes, procedures, regulation, and norms may lead to beneficial change. Risk making mistakes!

If we accept that mistakes are expected steps toward product or service improvement, then we should hold ourselves and others accountable. There should be "no place to hide" in our organization. Mistakes should be acknowledged so everybody can profit by them. Each of us—and our associates—is paid to contribute to the long-term financial viability of the business. This means appraising the performance of our people honestly and skillfully.

Microscopic Honesty

It pays to be honest about mistakes. It pays off in increased self-esteem, better job performance and increased confidence in the process of risk-taking. Not too long ago I watched professional leaders stand, one at a time, in front of a group and tell, while laughing about it, one of the most laughable mistakes of their careers—wrecked forklifts, customers waiting for parts mailed to the wrong addresses, incorrect glass dimension, handrails too high, and on and on they went. I watched as they were bonded and I observed with the telling of each experience the power of admitting faults and foibles. One class member, who now manages the maintenance department responsible for maintaining dozens of pieces of earth-moving equipment, told about the time when he started a forklift years ago only to discover painfully a minute later that there was no oil in the engine.

As I watched, I learned, once again, of the personal power we have when we just admit and laugh at our mistakes, our errors. Cover-up and posturing erodes our character and confidence and undermines our ability to lead. Today, practice microscopic honesty. Admit your errors and mistakes. You'll gain the confidence of others. You'll feel a load lifted. You'll have a new joy, enthusiasm, and life will be a lot more fun.

The admission of mistakes is a step toward fuller maturity in the individual. We have to be grownup to say, "Hey, I goofed." then go on to other things with the experience to backup the promise to yourself that you won't make the same mistake again.

Organizations which give their team players the latitude to make mistakes, as the normal process of producing a product or service, provide a working atmosphere that encourages more individual freedom of expression by a policy that does not condemn or criticize for predictable errors. Far from condoning negligence, such a policy encourages experimentation from which new ideas spring—mistakes are the parents of new products and services.

o   o   o

When You Blow It Show It

"Experience has two things to teach:
The first is that we must correct a good deal;
The second, that we must not correct too much."
Delacroix

Those best can bear reproof
Who merit praise.
Alexander Pope

It is much easier to be critical
Than to correct.
Benjamin Disraeli

$$>>>14$$

Direction Through Correction

"There is no right way to do a wrong thing."
Author Unknown

Sometimes, it appears, life does not work out. They said it would be here Tuesday, and it is not. You wanted those contracts signed, and they are not. You were set to go on vacation and the budget committee tells you there are problems and you are needed at the meetings.

Upsets are a part of our lives. To be empowered, we must learn to move through upsets quickly so they do not interfere with the achievement of our goals. We do not enter into working relationships to become upset. How do upsets develop? Upsets are usually a function of expectations not being met. At the source of most unfulfilled expectations is lack of clarity about what exactly was expected by whom, from whom and by when.

Usually, our first reaction in dealing with upsets is to find fault with the person who did not meet our expectations. We make a silent evaluation of that person's character or competence and avoid interaction to avoid further upset. This generally leads to gossip, condemnation and dissatisfaction. If we look at the ownership of the expectation more closely, we discover the responsibility for the expectation is retained by the person who created and communicated it in the first place. If the expectation is yours, then it is your responsibility as an empowering leader to see that it is met, especially if you are meeting the expectation through other people. The chain of events to avoid upsets looks like this:

1. Become clear about the specifics of your expectation.
2. Find someone with whom to entrust the achievement.
3. Clearly communicate the specifics of the expectation.
4. Check to see if the receiver understood the specifics.
5. Ask the receiver to accept responsibility for fulfilling the expectation.
6. Secure a promise to that effect...and receive true delivery of the expectation.

There are several links in this communication chain and when a breakdown occurs there is always the tendency to blame the other person. The act of blaming eliminates the possibility of correcting the breakdown from our position in the relationship. If either the sender or the receiver decides the other in the interaction is ineffective the situation becomes hopeless. If, on the other hand, either party takes 100 percent responsibility to make the situation work and holds the other person not responsible, the situation can be corrected. People holding themselves 100 percent responsible examine where they did not effectively implement one or more of the links in the communication chain. The question is *always,* "What can *I* bring to the interaction to make it work?"

Dishes

While it is a simple demonstration, the following anecdote shows how expectations may be conveyed to avoid upsets:

Cliff asked his daughter to do the dishes. She told him she had done them. He checked the dishwasher and it was still full. His immediate reaction was to do the thing you and I have done too often, which was to allow himself to go out of control. To become upset. After he regained control, he asked his daughter to come in and have a visit with him. They talked about the standard for cleaning dishes, what that standard looked like and entered into what Cliff described as a contract—the contract being that she would not begin watching television until she'd not only loaded the dishwasher but until the dishes were completed and she'd emptied the dishwasher again.

Withholding

Frequently, people hold back communication about what is not working out of a desire to be liked or to avoid the possibility of rejection—in other words, to preserve the relationship. Closer examination reveals that withholding upsets kills a relationship very quickly. Without relating what it's all about there is no relationship. When we hold back our negative thoughts, we carry them around and view the person we have withheld them from through a special pair of glasses tinted by our judgements. "I can't ask Leo to do this, he never gets anything back on time." Soon, we discover we have less and less to say to the person we have withheld from, and ultimately write the person off as a non-contributing member of the team and there is even more hopelessness about the situation.

The cost of withholding communication about upsets is your relationship with people. Put yourself in the position of the one who is not communicated with. When you have egg on your face do you want people to think those nasty things we think about people with egg on their faces? And worse yet, do you want them to talk to each other about that egg on *your* face? When a team is committed to each member and the members to the whole in true partnership, people are willing to say and listen to anything about one another. Two tools critical in handling upsets are Corrections and Reprimands. Correction is feedback regarding the unsuccessful fulfillment of expectations when the person did not know how to fulfill the expectation. It is given with the intention of teaching people what they are not fully able to deliver to the desired standard. A reprimand is feedback regarding the unsuccessful fulfillment of expectations when the person did know how to fill the expectation. It is delivered with the intention of having people perform up to their previously demonstrated capability.

Specialist

There are effective ways to make corrections work. I discovered some when Rob told our Leadership Development Lab about the specialist who came on the job site of a construction project which had been going extremely well—then nothing was the same from that day on.

The specialist has been on the company staff for four years. He was able, in one week, to completely upset the entire crew and, as a result, the job's progress. He completely turned off 12 guys who had been working successfully as a team until *he* showed up.

Rob took him aside to correct his behavior. The specialist's response was, "I do a good job." Rob said, "You do a *part* of your job well. When you upset the entire team and cause disharmony, you're not doing all of your job well."

Regardless of the uniqueness or special expertise someone brings to a job, it is never so important that we can sacrifice team effort for their contribution. The "artist," the "star," the "prima donna" cannot be justified in the decade of the 90s, regardless of their position, tenure or special expertise.

The questions: Why had this behavior been permitted to exist for four years, and how valuable is a person (regardless of his special expertise) who upsets and disrupts the entire team?

The answer: There's no excuse for permitting disruptive, unacceptable, upsetting behavior to persist for four years or for four months. Anyone who upsets the team in 1993 must be corrected or removed from the team.

This kind of constructive confrontation isn't easy. Few of us like to do it. We prefer to think that unacceptable behavior:

• Will go away.
• Doesn't make any difference anyway.
• Is something we can't do anything about.

This is disempowerment—we "rationalize" that it doesn't make that big a difference, that we can't help it or that people should ignore the jerk's behavior. We are acting out disempowered behavior and through the process are disempowering the entire team.

There are five tools of empowering feedback. Leaders are responsible for demonstrating leadership by—

... Encouraging extra effort when the team is challenged.

... Acknowledging performance and giving approval.

... Coaching team members to become more proficient.

... Correcting team members when they perform inadequately.

... Reprimanding team members when their performance shows inattention.

From what we know about this story, the disruptive specialist Rob reprimanded needed to be brought up sharp—focusing on his behavior that wasn't working, getting agreement that it is not working, getting a commitment to change and following up to be sure the change has been made and that the change is permanent. *Look* for the changed behavior. *Encourage* positive changes. If change does not occur, replace with an able and willing player.

The action I call you to is: Take a hard look at the behaviors of all your team members, and accept your responsibility to the team not to permit anyone to upset synergistic teamwork.

Confrontation

Confrontation is not easy. As Lillian Glass, author of *Say It ... Right: How To Talk In Any Social Or Business Situation,* says, "The key is respect. Yes, you're hurt. But after you've let out your point of view, you have to allow the other person the dignity to find a solution and make it work."

"Life," says Glass, "is full of awkward moments. No one has taught us how to handle them. We were brought up not to make waves, but society is simply to sophisticated today for that kind of response."

Instead:
- Confront now, not later.
- Be honest and diplomatic ("Donald Trump telling Larry King on national television that his breath smelled was not tactful.") Never correct in public.
- Treat relatives at least as well as you would strangers or co-workers ("It's your family that loves you, that will be at your bedside if you're sick, that will cry at your funeral.")
- Getting along with a rival. If the latest round of company promotions has left you butting heads with your nemesis, try this to help clear the air: "Look, we have an obvi-

ous personality difference, but we're stuck together. Let's afford each other the professional respect we deserve. Let's especially not belittle or badmouth each other. It's not in the best interests of the company."

In essence whatever competing you do on company time should be with yourself. After all, she says, "You can't be a perfect judge of another person or a particular situation because you don't know the nuances that go into it."

Avoid Dogmatic Declarations

Avoid dogmatic declaration, such as saying:
"As far as I'm concerned ..." or
"This is the way it is." or
"That's absurd." or
"That would never work." or
"That's the craziest idea I've ever heard."

Dogmatic declaration make others defensive and close the door to understanding, cooperation, and creativity. Do not give orders to try and prove who is boss. If you have to prove who is boss, you are not. People, like boats, toot loudest when they're in a fog.

Develop the habit of saying:
"What is your opinion?"
"How do you feel?"
"What do you think?"
"What would you do?"
"It seems to me ..."
"It appears ..."
"As far as I can tell ..."
"It looks to me like ..."

Avoid Arguments

Most arguments end with each "boxer" more firmly convinced than before that they are absolutely right. You can not win an argument. If you lose the argument, you have lost.If you win an argument, you lose because you lose a relationship and encourage your opponent to feel inferior. You hurt their pride, they will resent you and you lose the cooperation you wanted. Hardly a way to build an empowered team.

Whatever tactics successful leaders adopt in leading people, we find that the best leader's first and foremost rule is to avoid arguments. Their strategy is to use caution in handling opposition, and influence others by appealing to their wants. Above all, remember that an argument is often harmful and nearly always useless. Try to induce people to accept your idea without forcing them to admit that they themselves have been in the wrong. We are not suggesting that you concede important points. When you find it necessary to disagree, do so agreeably.

"Education is the ability to listen to almost anything without losing your temper or your self-confidence."
Robert Frost.

Ralph Waldo Emerson said, "If I do not believe as you believe, and you do not believe as I believe, all it shows is that I don't believe as you believe and you don't believe as I believe." Too wordy? Try, "I understand what you are saying," or "Try to look at it from my point of view for a moment," or "I respect what you are saying, and here may be another way of looking at it," or "I want us to work this out. Let's see if we can find some common ground."

Begin With Yes, Yes

The first step in persuading and leading people is to present your plans so that you get a "Yes Response" at the very start. Throughout your presentation, especially at the beginning, get as many "Yes's" as you possibly can. Begin by discussing the points on which you agree. Emphasize that you are striving for the same end and that your only difference may be one of method, not of purpose. When people are saying "Yes," they are moving forward, accepting, with an open attitude. The more "Yes's" we can get, the more likely we are to succeed in securing their cooperation and support for our ultimate proposal. When they are saying "Yes," they are listening. When we get a "No," they are thinking about why they are right.

"Get your adversary saying 'Yes, yes,' immediately!"
Socrates

Negotiation

Make a point of considering in advance the resistance that others may offer. Look at their objections as wants and needs that may interfere with what you want to do. Take those wants and needs into account when you make your plans. If possible, modify your proposals to satisfy them. In any event, prepare yourself ahead of time to deal with their opposition. When you encounter objections or resistance of any kind, ask yourself this question: "Can the point be conceded without risking my main purpose?" When you are bringing people around to your way of thinking, make as many "minor concessions" as you can.

If you are up against strong resistance to your main point, you might be wise to delay the issue. This gives the other person a chance to reconsider and provides you with an opportunity to reorganize your campaign. Under ordinary conditions, advance your ideas in a modest way that invites agreement—not in the pushy manner that provokes opposition.

To steer clear of arguments, avoid topics likely to cause a dispute. Try to listen silently when others attempt to force ideas upon you that you do not agree with.

When you deal with subordinates, make it easy for those with a complaint to see you and let them know that you are ready and eager to listen to them. Be accessible. By being accessible, you will keep little things from blowing out of proportion.

"He who argues is not a good man."
Lao Tzu

Tough Love

Iris, a recent Leadership Development Lab graduate, told us one of the most fantastic stories I've ever heard and it demonstrates how a level-headed approach can avoid disempowering breakdowns. About four years ago, as she was cleaning her 15-year-old son's bedroom, she discovered something that forced her to recognize that he was probably fooling around with dope. She found a note that he'd passed to someone else complaining about being straight for three days because it was a three-day weekend. When she confronted him, he said, "What do you think you can do about it?"

She took him to school, she waited outside his class, walked him to the next class, waited out side the class, and walked him to the next class. She kept up this routine for three months. When she shared this story with our class, she said, "Fortunately, I was self-employed."

I would say, it was fortunate for her son that she was

determined to apply what we call 'tough love' to help him know that, regardless of his complaint, or how he tried to make her feel, or how she might have felt, she was going to do what she had to do to save him form his addiction and she was not going to be upset about it.

I wonder what a different world this world would be if today there were more mothers like Iris. What about you? What's your level of commitment? What are you willing to do to handle difficult problems without being upset? How far are you willing to go to support, stand behind those you love? Tough love takes courage, determination, commitment and the willingness to do whatever it takes to help others you love live up to their best.

Partner

Yesterday morning, along with Bill Peckham, I conducted an introduction to a Partnering Event for the Associated General Contractors in Seattle, Washington. The room was filled, and people just kept filing in, one after another. These contractors had shown up to see if there really is a alternative to confrontation and litigation—the ultimate conclusion of the upsets carried to a legal ending. At the end of the meeting the senior contractor in the room came up to me and said, "I've been a general contractor for 36 years. I've spent more money on legal fees in the past three years than in the first 33 years. There has to be a better way.

Isn't it time for you and I to find ways to be agreeable, to find win-win solutions to problems before they are blown all out of proportion? Isn't it time for us to find ways to disagree in agreeable ways, to end disputes before they're out of control? Well there are ways to resolve upsets and to avoid them. David's story is one example:

Shirts

David, the president of a major Willamette Valley professional landscape company, told our Leadership Development Lab:

"It was midmorning on August 28 when I showed up at one of our jobsites in West Linn. Gary, the foreman, and his crew were already quite busy on the project. It was a beautiful, sunny summer morning; I could tell it was going to be a hot one. After I had finished setting up the crew with a few changes and some special customer requests, I jumped in my pickup truck and drove off.

"Then I remembered I hadn't posted one of our promotional 'Landscaping by ...' yard signs at the jobsite. When I returned to the site, only 20 to 30 minutes later, the crew had already taken off their company uniform shirts. This is a direct policy violation and they know it. Our company shirts are made of soft, light-weight fabric specially designed to breathe well. They are loose around the neck to help the workers stay cool on hot summer days.

"When the crew saw my pickup heading their way, the shirts went back on immediately and the crew scattered. When I approached Gary, he knew what was coming.

"Rather than point out the obvious policy violation, I tried a positive and constructive approach. Correction by direction. I decided to begin by getting in step. I complimented Gary on the crew's progress and the quality of the great landscape job they had already completed that morning. I acknowledged Gary for his 15 successful years with the company and pointed out how the crew looks up to him as an example. Then I reminded him of the reason of the shirt policy—that it makes the crew and the company look professional. I pointed out that the shirts were selected because they add to the client's sense of security, builds the team's self-esteem and especially because they are comfortable to wear even on August days.

"Gary seemed to accept what I said about the importance of wearing the uniforms and showed respect for my request that the uniform shirt policy be followed. We haven't had a problem with compliance since.

"The lesson I learned is: It pays to be positive. I need to always get in step with my team and point out their strengths even when my first response might be to let them have it."

The actions I call you to are:

1. Be sure you have good reasons for all of your policies.
2. Strive for as few policies as possible.
3. Look for ways to make your policies win-win; win for your customer, win for your employees, win for your company.
4. Take the time to explain the reasons for, and benefits of all your company's rules and policies. Remember when talking about policies to always answer the ever-present "WIFM" question—What's In It For Me?

The benefit you will gain is the "willing cooperation" of your team. You will present a consistent and unified front; you will look good to your customers, the public; and the self-esteem of your team will grow. Plus, you will reduce turnover and retain customers.

Effective Feedback

The method to resolve upsets I use is called feedback. David's story is a good example of feedback in action. Following are recommendations for creating effective feedback:

Feedback to be empowering must be specific rather

than general. To be told that you are "dominating" is not as useful as "Just now you were not listening to what the others said, but I felt I had to agree with your arguments or face attack from you."

Feedback is focused on behavior rather than on the person. It is important that we refer to what people do rather than to what we think or imagine they do. It is more useful to say that a person "talked more than anyone else in this meeting" rather than that she is a "loudmouth." The first statement allows for the possibility of change; the second implies a fixed personality trait. Most certainly the second statement will result in a defensive reaction from the accused person.

Feedback takes into account the needs of the receiver of the feedback. Feedback can be destructive when it serves only our own needs and fails to consider the needs of the person on the receiving end. It should be given to help, not to hurt. Too often we give feedback because it makes us feel better or gives us a psychological advantage.

Empowering feedback is directed toward behaviors the receiver can do something about. You increase others' frustration when you remind them of some shortcomings over which they feel they have no control or a physical characteristic that they can do nothing about.

Empowering feedback is solicited rather than imposed. Feedback is most useful when the receiver asks the questions that those observing him can answer.

Feedback involves sharing of information rather than giving advice. Information is power. By sharing information, we leave people free to decide for themselves, in accordance with their own goals, needs and aspirations. When we give advice to people, we tell them what to do, and unless asked for, this advice may be viewed as criticism. If feedback is not openly solicited, you as the empowering leader can simply ask: "Would you like feedback on your effectiveness in this meeting, or would you like some coaching on your involvement in our negotiation?"

How can I be more effective?

How can I make better use of my time?

How can I make our meeting more productive?

Feedback is well-timed. In general, immediate feedback is most useful (depending, of course, on the person's readiness to hear it and support available from others). The reception and use of feedback involves many possible emotional reactions. Excellent feedback presented at an inappropriate time may not be very helpful at all.

Empowering feedback involves the amount of information the receiver can use rather than the amount we would like to give. To overload people with feedback is to reduce the possibility that they can effectively use it. When we give more than can be used, more often that not we are satisfying some need of our own rather than empowering the other person.

Feedback concerns what is said or done or how, but not why. The "why" takes us from what we observe to the land of inferences and assumptions. It makes us "psycho-pests." Guessing at people's motivations or intentions tends to alienate them and increases resentment, suspicion and distrust; it does not contribute to learning or development. It is dangerous to assume that we know why people say or do something, or what they are "really" trying to accomplish. However, if we are uncertain of other's motives or intent, this uncertainty itself is feedback and should be revealed.

"Is there some reason why you have been late for our staff meetings the last three days? Also, I noticed how you rolled your eyes when I asked for ideas on how to improve safety on the project."

Feedback is checked to ensure clear communication.

One method is to have the receiver rephrase the feedback just received to see if it corresponds to what the sender has in mind. No matter what the intent, feedback can be threatening and easily distorted.

Coaching To Build People And Make Them Successful

Try coaching people to improve their performances and to come up with ideas of their own to make the organization work better.

Take a look at the possible responses to a person's attempted performance:

1. You can laugh at the performance.
2. You can point out the obvious error or mistake.
3. You can praise followed by destructive "But ..."
4. You can over-kill with corrective feedback.
5. Or you can coach to help people improve their performance. People listen when you are complimentary and they feel it is possible that you can assist them.

There are three simple steps to raising the confidence of team members.

1. Tell them what they did well.
2. Show them one easy way they can improve their performance.
3. Predict their success and you will be surprised at the positive outcome.

Repeat these three steps with more and more finely-tuned coaching, as the person's skills increase, until they reach the desired performance.

Coaching and correcting are an art. Like any other art form, they take practice, patience and courageous action. Here are some guidelines for coaching and correcting people, and getting them to thank you for it.

1. Begin with "effective approval" ... (*and* versus *but*)
2. Talk about their errors indirectly.
3. Talk about your own errors first.
4. Ask questions, do not order them.
5. Do not embarrass them.
6. Give approval to the smallest improvement and every improvement.
7. Give them a positive reputation to live up to.
8. Encourage their improvement.
9. Make them feel good about what you want them to do by:
    ... Knowing in advance exactly what you expect of the other person.
    ... Asking yourself what it is they really want.
    ... Thinking what benefits they will get from doing what you want.
    ... Matching those benefits to their wants.

Direction through correction is an important part of human interaction. The empowering leader learns how to make needed changes in the thinking and performance of his team by using tools of communication in a fashion that influences the outcome of negotiations by introducing techniques of approval, encouragement and corrective feedback. Used effectively, the feedback tools the empowering leader brings into play smooth over upsets and pave the way to understanding, cooperation and synergistic performance of everyone involved.

o   o   o

Avoid Dogmatic Declarations
Avoid Arguments
Begin With Yes, Yes

A Winner Or A Loser?

A Winner says, "let's find out;" a Loser says, "Nobody knows."

When a Winner makes a mistake, he say, "I was wrong."

When a Loser makes a mistake, he says, "It wasn't my fault."

A Winner isn't nearly as afraid of losing as a Loser is secretly afraid of winning.

A Winner works harder than a Loser and has more time.

A Loser is always "too busy" to do what is necessary.

A Winner goes through a problem.

A Loser goes around it and never gets past it.

A Winner makes commitments.

A Loser makes promises.

A Winner shows he's sorry by making up for it.

A Loser says, "I'm sorry," but does the same thing the next time.

A Winner knows what to fight for and what to compromise on.

A Loser compromises on what he shouldn't and fights for what isn't worth while fighting about.

A Winner listens.

A Loser just waits until it's his turn to talk.

A Winner feels strong enough to be gentle.

A Loser is never gentle—he's either weak or pettily tyrannous by turns.

A Winner says, "There ought to be a better way to do it."

Excerpt from

Are You A Winner Or Loser

Sidney Harris

Practical Problem Solving

"Some men have thousands of reasons
Why they cannot do what they want to,
When all they need is one reason they can."

Willis R. Whitney

The object of this chapter is to present methods to acknowledge problems, encourage people to report problems, and discuss methods to solve problems. Before we look at the problem-solving process, let's examine the philosophy of good problem-solvers. Excellent companies recognize that every problem represents an opportunity for learning and improvement. Companies which are not doing well are complacent or practice transferring blame to others when problems arise. Creating a philosophy of continuous improvement through "creative dissatisfaction" helps us embrace the opportunities which problems offer.

Somehow, we have accepted the idea that problems reflect inadequacies in people. This attitude creates an atmosphere that is conductive to blame placing when a problem arises. It must be Bill's fault for not anticipating it.

Problems are normal; all companies deal with problems. The difference between a good company and an excellent company is how it approaches, solves and learns from problems.

Meltdown

Kirk, the maintenance manager for a Portland-area manufacturer, told the following story at our Leadership Development Lab:

"We experienced a major meltdown in the plant this last week. It wasn't the first time, and it was just as bad as ever, but there was something different this time. The difference was the way I handled it. This time, I responded instead of reacting."

Reacting, remember, is when we act without thinking—it's a knee-jerk action.

Kirk responded by not losing his temper. Instead of losing his temper, trying to point out who was wrong, fixing blame on a person, this time he focused his attention on trying to discover the root cause of the problem, trying to find out how or where the system failed.

Hollering and yelling sets up a scenario: you react, then they react in defense. This series of reactions eliminates any possibility for significant, permanent and continuous performance improvement.

It's in responding, not reacting, that we cause people to become open, willing to talk about problems, willing to admit problems exist, willing and able (at the lowest level in the organization) to become problem-solvers. When we include people closest to the problem in our pursuit of the solution, we make them more aware of how they can keep problems from occurring. This helps all the members of the team to be open and responsive.

The empowering leader's role is to create a culture where everyone is committed to continuous improvement and where defensiveness is replaced with responsiveness. How can you do this? You must communicate your commitment to Continuous Improvement and Superior Customer Service.

You also must create an environment where, when problems occur, people know that it's okay to say, "I think we've got a problem," instead of waiting for things to blow completely out of proportion. Instead of waiting for someone else to report the problem, people at the the lowest possible level feel empowered to say, "Whoops, I think something's not working."

Simple, yet it is not the traditional approach that has been taken by most organizations. To often in the past, we have killed the messenger who has informed us of the problem. It's important for us to recognize those times in our culture when we have killed the messenger.

Top managers (dominant, dynamic individuals) can kill the messenger and send the signal "Keep your head down" with small comments like: "You know better than that." "I can't believe you let that happen." "What's wrong with you, anyway?"

To turn the culture around—to make a 180-degree turn—make heroes out of the people who report the problem, not just the people who solve the problem. Empower the people who are closest to the problems early in the process versus late in the life cycle of the process.

Why wait until you have passed through a half-dozen value-added stages to say, "This is wrong, this won't work." Worse yet, why wait for the customer to complain, return a defective item and/or ask for a credit?

By empowering your team to stop the process, "shut down the line," you may be amazed at how many errors you begin to eliminate, how much money you save and how you positively impact morale. This is empowering leadership. It is problem solving in the best and most efficient way.

The Problem Statement

My experience shows that 75 percent of us will write the cause or solution to a problem when we are asked to come up with a definition of the problem. We prescribe medicine or recommend an operation *before* we've named the problem, described it and long before we have found the cause.

For example, you walk into your kitchen at home after attending a movie. There on the floor is an inch of water; the sink is overflowing, and no one else is there. A stack of dishes is in the sink, apparently blocking the drain. Which of the following is the definition of the problem:

1. Turn off the water.
2. The drain is blocked.
3. Somebody left the kitchen with the water running.
4. Unexpectedly, there is an inch of water on the floor.

The first is an appropriate action, a decision really, to solve the problem, but it is not a definition of the problem. Turn the faucet off and you've still got water on the floor and a sink that can't be used.

The second is a cause statement. It does not describe the problem, but leaps right to a cause, which may or may not be the real cause. At any rate, it too is not a statement of the problem.

Number three represents preventive action to head off problems like this, but it won't help us with this problem we have right now.

The fourth is a definition of the problem. It says what is actually happening, which was not expected, and for which you are not sure of the cause.

Just like an accurate diagnosis by a capable doctor a

problem statement identifies what is wrong. As the first step, it focuses on what is, not on why it got that way or how to fix it. Following is a simple model to put the problem-solving process on track:

1. What is the problem? How do we know when a problem exists? A problem exists when things are no longer *ideal.* A problem is anything that stands between you and your steady progress toward your goals. *An inch of water on the floor indicates a serious problem, and blocks your goal of convenient, safe maintenance-free living.*

2. A problem well-stated is a problem half-solved! Accurately define the problem. Make sure to separate symptoms from the real problem. State your problem in "Problematical" terms—one statement, not a question. In the statement of your problem, do not include the cause of the problem or the solution to the problem.

3. Open yourself to all *possible* causes of the problem. Brainstorm the possible causes: This will allow your team to identify as many possible causes without judging why they exist and who they influence. The brainstorming approach will eliminate the CYA defensive coverup tactics. It will also permit the team to ultimately identify the real cause among all those examined.

4. The team will generate a multiplicity of possible solutions to the problem. Here we want quantity, not quality. No judgment of the person or solution being presented.

5. After the team has generated all possible solutions they will identify the best possible solution. This can be best accomplished through consensus or majority-vote decision-making.

6. Put the solution into action and determine what actions must be taken to implement the solution. Identify who is responsible to implement the action plan, how the action plan

will be implemented, and when. You must take action, or all of the forethought and work goes down the drain. Another wasted meeting.

7. Make sure the people affected by the solution are willing to cooperate. This problem-solving process leads to unified action on the part of the team. Involve your team in the above process and your solutions will be accepted and acted upon.

Fixing The Cause

What does a mechanic do when you take your car for a visit? He asks you questions. He probes, tests, wiggles things, trying to find the cause of the symptoms. That's just what we need to do here. Try hard not to jump to causes—take time to strip away your prejudices, hunches, attitudes, suspicions. Just let the questions flow.

In the case of the overflowing sink, just walking over to it will suggest some causes. The unwashed dishes blocking the drain is one cause. But observation has its limits. Since there are often spectators in front of a house on fire, you might think one of them set the fire. Likewise, cottage cheese seems to cause overweight, since fat people seem to eat a lot of it.

Drip, Drip, Drip

When I finally started my 1978 500CX motorcycle one morning not too long ago, it sounded sweet. I hadn't really ridden it for three years. I wanted to restore it to original. I put a lot of time in it earlier this summer. Just when I had it pieced back together I discovered a leak in the gas tank. I didn't know what to do. I didn't know anyone who had a shop that does that kind of work. I knew it could be expensive, potentially explosive, and a new gas tank was completely out of the question. I put the project on hold for several weeks.

I visited a local auto parts store on the off chance that they might have a liquid way of repairing it. To tell you the truth, I was a little out of my comfort zone even asking about it.

Well, of course they offered me three specific options for repair, all were easy, effective, safe and inexpensive.

The lesson I learned from this experience is that I must explore alternative solutions to problems I've never considered. I must reframe my problem if I'm gong to find new, innovative solutions to old, troublesome problems. I must go beyond the nine dots.

Today, as you're facing problems, as you're attempting continuous improvements in processes, methods, cooperation, reframe your problem, form a new paradigm, explore beyond your old references. Old references keep us trapped in the past. Look at options you've never considered, and ask "What if?" You'll find easier, safer, faster, more cost-effective ways to solve your problems.

Second Opinion

Not too long ago, we asked Stacy over to our house to look at some carpenter repair work we needed to have done. Stacy's a pro. I've seen some of his work. He specializes in rehab house repair work. His ideas for fixing our deck more closely matched what I had originally thought I needed to do and will require less time and money than the approach reflected in the first estimate we received.

The lesson I learned from this experience is to get a second opinion, to listen to my instincts. The benefit you will gain when you open yourself to outside multiple solutions is more productive action. You'll move further faster. You'll reach your goals easier.

Your job as the empowering leader of any problem-solving conference is not to solve the problem or come up with the ideas. Your job is to be sure you generate the maximum number of ideas from everyone in your group and to be sure the ideas are understood. To gain maximum involvement here are a few suggestions:

1. Make certain that everyone in your group participates. If you have someone who is holding back, ask, "Joe, what do you think?"

2. Never permit criticism, evaluation, or judgement when you are collecting ideas.

3. Use neutral tones when you ask, "How would that work?" "How do you mean that?" "Can you give us an example?"

4. Original thought must be stimulated or you will remain stuck in the conventionality of the past. Include outsiders—people from outside your department, area or company. Ask someone who is blissfully ignorant of why it can't be done to participate in your meeting. Invite people to participate who don't have a personal stake in the outcome.

5. By encouraging wild ideas, you develop useable innovations.

6. Keep the vision of the desired outcome or destination always in front of the team so it cannot forget what it is striving for.

7. Problem-solving is endless. You must never stop exploring for better ways. This insures continuous improvement. This effort, this skill is one of the most important ones your team can develop.

Maintenance Plan

Now is the time for the team to decide what steps can be taken to avoid the problem in the future. It's like a dental maintenance plan, when the dentist suggests you floss more, or brush more, or tells you to quit smoking or you'll stain your teeth permanently.

The dentist diagnosed your problem, found the cause, decided on treatment. Then he developed your treatment plan. It worked, and he wants to help you keep your teeth healthy.

If you are going to espouse problem solving, it's extremely important that you make it clear to every member of your team that "we will keep our commitments, and we'll renegotiate deadlines when deadlines can't be met." As I point out in my book, *Repeat Business,* "Excuses don't look good on me." Any time we find ourselves not able to keep our commitments, the next thing we find ourselves doing is making up excuses.

To achieve Total Quality Leadership, impeccable records of quality must be kept, including the number of promises made, percentage of goods shipped on time, back orders, orders searched for, requests not kept, merchandise asked for that you don't stock and information that was needed which you weren't able to provide to customers.

By tracking the percentage of promises fulfilled and striving to continually improve our performance, we build empowered teams that deliver, and we anticipate problems before they develop.

Problem-Solving Five Steps

"You can not solve a problem until you admit you have one."

State the Problem (the obstacle to goal achievement) in one sentence. Remember, this statement does not include the cause of the problem, the solution, and it is never stated as a question.

Problem:_____
_____
_____
_____

What are some of the *possible* causes? (Brainstorm)
_____
_____
_____
_____

What are some of the *possible* solutions. (Brainstorm)
_____
_____
_____
_____

What is the best solution, considering the resources, time and people available?
_____
_____
_____
_____

What action must be taken to implement the solutions?
When: _____
Who: _____
How:_____

Never end a meeting without assigning a responsible person to implement the decision reached during the meeting.

How To Acquire The Habit Of Decisiveness

We must acquire the habit of making decisions. We must dispose rapidly of the dozens of little problems that come up every day. The way to do that is to make decisions. Right or wrong, make decisions!

It is not important to make the correct decision. What matters is to make the decision. Make it. Force yourself on to the next one rather than getting stuck in worrying about whether your decisions was "right." This is the only way you can acquire the rare habit of making decisions. Once we acquire this habit, we step into the top 10 percent of American "doers," the top leaders.

A man or woman on the firing line of decision making can't do anything but win! Sound judgment is acquired only by the habit of decision making. We learn from experience and the outcome of our decisions, but we must start making decisions *now*. We must *act*, and act *quickly!*

Decision Making

Not all decisions we make are tied to problems. Starting new ventures, exploiting unforeseen opportunities and achieving continuous improvement requires "new decisions." Every decision does not have a critical factor which must be corrected or changed. At it's simplest level, decision-making means choosing one solution of several choices.

Make The Decision Effective

Consider those who will have to make the decision effective. Answer the following questions:

A. How long will it take to make the decision effective?

_____

_____

B. What minimum training will be needed to effect the solution?

_____

_____

I can't leave the subject of problem solving without asking you to adopt the philosophy apparent in the following two ideas. They are dynamite:

Eat problems for lunch. We need to consider the situations that arise in our work areas as opportunities for improvement rather than as headaches or distractions. Problems can be our best teachers if we are open to working with them rather than simply trying to "solve" them. In addition, we need to communicate this positive attitude to our associates.

Eliminate "either/or thinking." We cannot let ourselves think of an action as either being for our owners or for our people. We need action that serves both. We cannot let ourselves think in terms of having either high quality or low cost. We need action that accomplishes both. In *Future Perfect,* Stanley Davis argues that leaders "who can hold opposites in their vision simultaneously can win the kingdom."

> *Problems are only opportunities*
> *In work clothes.*
>> Henry J. Kaiser

> *Our problems are man-made,*
> *Therefore they may be solved by man.*
> *And man can be as big as he wants.*
> *No problem of human destiny is beyond human beings.*
>> John F. Kennedy

o   o   o

Analyze • Decide • Act

Life's Responsibilities

This is the thing I would have you learn:
Nothing is yours to keep.
And never you'll rest from the need of toil
'Til the last long final sleep.
There's never a place or a time in life
When nothing you'll have to do.
Whatever the post you shall come to here,
It shall call for the best in you.
You may dream of riches and all the joy
Which silver and gold can buy,
But the greater the wealth that may come to you
The greater your care shall lie.
For the more that this life shall give to you
The more to life you must give,
For this is the great unwritten law:
No man to himself can live.
As God bestowed on you talents rare
By which you may rise to fame,
Then upon your soul he has laid the charge
With courage to use the same.
Nor skill nor power can bring you ease,
For this you shall find is true:
He who has much to do with here
Shall ever have much to do.
For life and talents and wealth and fame
Are given to men in trust,
And each must work with the gifts he has
'Til his flesh returns to dust.
For this is the law which governs all,
And this is the common test:
He that shall come to the best life has
Must give to the world his best.
                              Edgar A.Guest

$$>>>16$$

Leaders Are Learners

"Nothing stops the man who desires to achieve.
Every obstacle is simply a course
To develop his achievement muscle.
It's a strengthening of his powers of accomplishment."
Eric Butterworth

I was very fortunate in 1960, early in my career, to hear
Earl Nightingale's classic presentation, "The Strangest Secret."
His message was that you are where your thoughts have brought
you. Your mind is like a fertile field; plant it with negative seeds
and you'll reap negative results. Plant it with positive seeds and
harvest joy, happiness and plenty. Nightingale made a great
impact on my life. I became a regular listener to his radio program, "Keys to Success." I was thrilled when I had the opportunity to hear him live at the Ford Auditorium in downtown
Detroit in 1962. During his talk, he said, "If you were investing
in a company for long-term growth, what kind would it be—one
in which you might buy stock and hold it for 20 or 30 years till
retirement"

As the audience pondered his question, he said, "I'd

recommend that you invest in a company that had a very active research and development, one that plows back at least ten percent of its earnings into new product development."

Then he went on to say, "You must have your own research and development department if you are going to be successful. Put ten percent of your income and time in your own personal growth and development and you'll be a success." His advice was some of the best I have ever heard and I have tried to live by it.

I'm urging you as a leader to set aside time to be a learner. Don't just wait for your company or association to send you to programs. Search outside of your industry, search outside of your association for good ideas to improve your abilities. Personal development and other kinds of training will stimulate your creativity which will bring you new thoughts and new opportunities.

All significant breakthroughs offer leaders as learners new paths to follow. The trick is to recognize them when they happen. Often when we are close to opportunities we are blind to them. Perhaps one of the most striking examples is the quartz watch invented by the Swiss. They were so sure it was worthless that they didn't bother to patent it. At that time, 80 percent of the world's watches were made by the Swiss, creating employment for lots of watch makers. Texas Instruments and Seiko happened to see the quartz watch invention at a trade show. They picked up the technology and the rest is history. Learning new ideas helps prepare us to be ready when innovations come along that offer opportunity. Most important, learn to learn from your own experiences. Force yourself to do what I have urged the members of my classes to do for decades: At the culmination of every significant event in your life, ask yourself this question: "What have I learned from this experience?"

At the close of every day, ask yourself, "What was the

single most important event in my day today, and what did I learn from it?"

Contacts

One afternoon recently I arrived at the Water Tower Eye Clinic for my annual eye examination. When I walked in, I was wearing glasses, bifocals. I stopped wearing my contacts a few months ago because it was just too much hassle to wear them, yet have to search for my reading glasses all the time for close up reading. So far as I could see there was only one answer. That was to start wearing my bifocal glasses again. I asked the doctor about bifocal contacts and he confirmed what I've heard—"They just don't seem to work very well." After my examination, he said, "Let's see how this works." He popped in a couple of contacts. I could see to read and I could see in the distance. What did he do? A new combination—a contact for one eye for reading, a contact for the other eye for distance. So far, so good. I'm wearing them today, I can read, I was able to write this message, and I can see to drive.

The lesson I learned is that in order for me to find improvements—better ways—I must open myself to all possibilities. I must be willing to see things differently, open my eyes, look around, wake up.

As empowering leaders, we have the responsibility to open our eyes to new possibilities, new answers to old problems, new combinations. Examine possibilities up close and take a hard look at them, push them away for new perspective. As you open yourself to new options and fresh combination, you'll find better and better ways to accomplish your objectives and goals. You'll experience continuous improvements, and that is what makes up an empowering leader.

Learn About The Players On Your Team

Alan told our Leadership Development Lab a story that illustrates the value of learning about the players on your team.

"In a conversation with one of my managers, I was tipped off that Carleen may have some feelings that I was treating her differently from others in our office. With this in mind, I made it a point to be proactive and talk with Carleen. I planned to force myself to really listen to her point of view without judgement. I followed the seven steps to effective listening. I urged her to be honest and express any feelings on her mind. She came back to me the next day to tell me how much better she felt and how much she appreciated my attention."

"I have resolved to be available and receptive to all of my team at all times, and really listen to what they have to say, and not waste time justifying, excusing or telling them why they are wrong. The lesson I learned is that by listening, being attentive, and getting to know everyone on my team, I am assured of genuine open and meaningful understanding and real communication. The action I call you to is: Find the time to have meaningful and open communication with your team. Have a one-on-one with everyone on your team this week. The benefits you will gain are apparent. You will improve your relationship with and create a more positive environment for all of your employees. You will be an empowering leader."

Leadership, and the job of the leader always to be a learner was defined for me by the words of Benjamin Barber who said:

"I don't divide the world into the weak and the strong, or the successes and the failures, those who make it or those who don't. I divide the world into learners and nonlearners.

"There are people who learn, who are open to what happens around them, who listen, who hear the lessons. When they do something stupid, they don't do it again. And when they do something that works a little bit, they do it even better with greater intensity the next time. The question to ask is not whether you are a success or a failure, but whether you are a learner or a nonlearner."

Not too long ago, a superintendent of schools in Oregon made a presentation I admired. He said to an audience of teachers, "We must stop trying to turn out students to fill specific jobs. The young people who are in our schools will not have just one job. Even though you and I may have chosen teaching early in our lives as a career and though we may stay in teaching all of our lives—doubtful though in this era of rapid change—our students will not. They'll have not one career but two, three, four, possible five. They will have careers in jobs that don't even exist today. We must help them learn how to learn."

You as a leader must learn how to learn. The old model of learning the job and then doing it for the rest of your life is as out-of-date as the manual typewriter, and the two-step photocopy machines I sold in the early sixties. Leaders are readers. Leaders are learners. This means that we are reading the magazines, other periodicals and books that relate directly to our field and those outside our field of interest, that relate to hobbies and avocations.

More importantly, leaders understand how necessary it is to take at least one meaningful self-development program each year. They understand that they must reinvest at least ten percent of their time in their own personal development and growth.

I was privileged for over 18 months to record a 45-second daily motivational message for people who phoned in to get a lift. It was a big job for me to find the kernel in each incident that inspired a message I passed on to others. This kind of learning is what I call "Authentic Learning." This is real learning.

Discussing your learning experience with others in your life at the close of your day can be one of the most empowering things you can do. When you've reached an understanding with yourself about what you've learned from special incidents in your life, sharing your understanding with others can help clarify your own learning.

Sometimes when we reach narrow, inappropriate conclusions based on our experiences, we repeat the same mistakes over and over. Of course, it's easier to notice repeated mistakes in others than in ourselves. But by forcing yourself to analyze each significant event that happens to you each day will ultimately help you learn more from your experiences.

Pushing yourself beyond your comfort zone is one of the most important things you can do to stimulate your learning. Taking risks, taking chances, going beyond where you're comfortable is the uncertain place where you really do your learning.

Natural Food

Benjamin Franklin set his personal standards high. He never let himself think that he had learned enough. This is explained by the author James Cousins who wrote:

"His education was in the nature of a chain reaction of discovery. After only a few years of formal elementary schooling, he began his explorations in thought and knowledge. One book pointed the way to sundry others; each subject had its own continuing mysteries and its challenges.

"The advantage of self-education in Franklin's case was clear. There were no boundary lines or terminal rituals, as in formal schooling, to mislead a person into thinking that he had completed his education. It never occurred to him that there was any point at which he could say that his learning was adequate for his life's work or for life itself. He could no more conceive of cutting his mind off from its natural food, knowledge, than he could expect to function physically in a starved condition. There was nothing phenomenal to him in the ability to think creatively and competently in so many fields; this was how the human mind was supposed to work."

Learning And Growing

Within every experience there is a lesson for us and others to learn. Although the possibility to learn from every experience exists, we actually learn from only a few. How can we change this? How do we turn our lives into a classroom, a laboratory to learn from and make every day another meaningful rung on the ladder to success?

1. We recognize that we have not been learning and growing at a pace acceptable to us.

2. We believe we *can* learn from all our experiences—those we call good and, best of all, those we aren't currently even aware of.

3. We take full *responsibility* for everything that happens in our lives. Not blaming others, circumstances, or powers outside of our control.

4. We look for the *lesson* for *us* in all our *experiences.*

5. We look for the principle operating beneath the experience. Part of this is believing we live in an orderly, consistent universe, a universe in which nothing happens by accident.

6. We express the experience and the lesson learned from it. Until we can verbalize or write about an experience, we haven't fully realized and understood the experience. We haven't truly "experienced the experience." An expression of the lesson learned will clarify and crystallize the experience so we can learn from and build on it.

Lobster

I found one of the most fascinating comments about
learning and risk in a statement Eda LeShan made in an article
she wrote for *Women's Day:*
"I recently celebrated my fifty-ninth birthday. As usual
I was utterly astounded by the passing of the years. It seems to
me that last year I was only twenty-five and the year before that
I was about twelve. But no matter how surprising they are, I find
birthdays useful. They remind me that I must not waste a minute
of my life—and that I must keep on growing and changing in
order to truly celebrate my birthdays.
"A number of years ago I wrote a book called *The
Wonderful Crisis Of Middle Age.* I thought middle age could be
called wonderful because it seemed to be a chance for a second
adolescence—a time during which I could make new and better
decisions about the rest of my life. While I was writing the book,
I met an oceanographer who asked if I knew how a lobster was
able to grow bigger when its shell was so hard. I had to admit
that learning how lobsters grow had never been high on my list
of priorities. But now that he had mentioned it, how in the world
could a lobster grow? The only way, he explained, is for the
lobster to shed its shell at regular intervals. When its body
begins to feel cramped inside the shell, the lobster instinctively
looks for a reasonable spot to rest while the hard shell comes off
and the pink membrane just inside forms the basis of the next
shell. But no matter where a lobster goes for this shedding
process, it is very vulnerable. It can get tossed against a coral
reef or eaten by a fish. In other words, a lobster has to risk its life
in order to grow.
"I found myself preoccupied with the lobster story for
days after hearing it. I finally realized that it was a symbol for
the book I was writing. The lobster could teach us that the only

way to endure the passage of time and the limits of our mortality is to know that we are growing and changing, that we are becoming more than we have been with each year of our lives.

"We all know when our shells have gotten too tight. We feel angry or depressed or frightened because life is no longer exciting or challenging. We are doing the same old things and beginning to feel bored. Or we are dong things we hate to do and are feeling stifled in our shells.

"Some of us continue to smother in old shells that are no longer useful or productive. That way we can at least feel safe—nothing can happen to us. Others are luckier; even though we know we will be vulnerable—that there are dangers ahead—we realize that we must take risks or suffocate.

"In honor of my birthday, I invite you to share the party I always go to—the one where I shed this year's shell, despite the dangers, in order to get ready for new and better adventures."

If you are a leader and you are growing, the test you have to make on yourself on every one of your own birthdays is to ask yourself if it is not time to stretch your mind "lobster-like" and reach for the next step in your personal growth. Stretching will keep you young and your mind flexible.

o   o   o

It was Aldous Huxley who wrote that "Experience is not what happens to a man. It's what a man does with what happens to him."

What Huxley said best demonstrates the necessity for the empowering leader to always be open to new ideas, improved ways of doing things, to new translations of old experiences, and to openness in his judgement of people.

"Do not be too timid and squeamish about your actions. All life is an experiment. The more experiments you make the better. What if they are a little coarse, and you may get your coat soiled or torn? What if you do fail, and get fairly rolled in the dirt once or twice? Up again, you shall never be so afraid of a tumble."

Ralph Waldo Emerson

o   o   o

Invest In The Best • Yourself

About The Author

Larry W. Dennis is the energetic founder of Turbo Management Systems. The author of the successful book, *Repeat Business,* and his new book, *Empowering Leadership,* shares the philosophy behind his ability to improve profits for hundreds of businesses whose key managers have learned the important principles of Empowering Leadership and Superior Customer Service. Dennis is the inventor of the patented video training system, Psycho-Actualized Learning, and is a dedicated father who has been profiled in "Secrets of Raising Teenagers Successfully." Dennis also serves on the Business Advisory Council of Warner Pacific College.

For more information about Turbo Management Systems, Management Team Advance, Cultural Quality awareness, Leadership Development Labs, or Team Management Training contact:

Turbo Management Systems™
5440 S. W. Westgate Drive, Suite 340
Portland, Oregon 97221
Telephone: 503-292-1919